BEYOND OATMEAL:

OATS - THE IMPRESSIVE SUPERFOOD

Beth Holm

Wise & Thrifty Book Series
Copyright © 2024 Beth Holm
All rights reserved.
Publisher BeeLovedHolm
ISBN 978-1-963278-05-7
June 2024

Table of Contents

The Oat Odyssey: A Journey of Health and Happiness

Introduction

Welcome to the wonderful world of oats - a versatile, nutritious, and sustainable Supergrain that has captured my heart and inspired my cooking journey. In "Beyond Oatmeal: Oats - The Impressive Superfood," I invite you to join me on a delicious exploration of oats' incredible benefits.

From creamy porridge and chewy granola bars to savory oat burgers and oat-tofu, oats can be transformed into a wide array of mouthwatering dishes that are as nourishing as they are satisfying. Not only are oats packed with essential nutrients like fiber, protein, and antioxidants, but they also have the power to support heart health, regulate blood sugar levels, and promote a healthy weight.

But my love for oats goes beyond their health benefits. I am deeply passionate about the sustainability of whole grain cooking and the remarkable qualities of this humble grain that have inspired me to create this book. Through the pages of "Beyond Oatmeal," I aim to share my knowledge, recipes, and tips for incorporating oats into your meals in creative and delicious ways.

Forty years ago, I began doing food storage co-op orders. I taught others that a good way to start accumulating food storage is to buy and use oats as the first step. By replacing cereal with oats, you can significantly reduce your grocery expenses. This initial investment in oats paves the way for a cycle of savings, enabling you to build your food storage with other whole food staples. Oats are not only cost-effective but also versatile, serving as a foundation for a variety of healthy meals. They are a blank canvas for creativity, ready to be enhanced with fruits, nuts, and seeds. 'Beyond Oatmeal' is a guide to incorporating oats into your diet in an economical and healthful way, transforming your approach to family nutrition. Let's explore the endless possibilities that oats offer in our daily lives.

Oats are naturally gluten-free, making them a suitable grain option for those with gluten sensitivities or celiac disease.

However, it's important to note that oats can often be contaminated with gluten. Oats are naturally gluten-free, making them a suitable grain option for those with gluten sensitivities or celiac disease. However, it's important to note that oats can often be contaminated with gluten during processing, as they are frequently processed in facilities that also handle wheat, barley, and rye. Oats processed in a certified gluten-free facility are labeled "gluten-free".

While creating my oat-centric recipes, I purposefully eliminated oils and sugars. Additionally, I've made salt optional, allowing for a substitution with miso. This is inspired by the principles of health authorities like Dr. Caldwell B. Esselstyn, Jr. (Esselstyn, n.d.), Dr. Dean Ornish (Ornish, n.d.), Dr. Joel Fuhrman (Fuhrman, n.d.), Dr. T. Colin Campbell (Campbell, n.d.), Dr. Michael Greger (Greger, n.d.), and Dr. John McDougall (McDougall, n.d.). These experts promote a diet rich in whole foods devoid of added sugars oils, and salt to enhance heart health and avert chronic illnesses. The logic is straightforward: high intake of added sugars is associated with increased risks of fatty liver, type 2 diabetes, and heart disease. Likewise, eliminating oils can lead to reduced inflammation and better heart health. Since embracing this lifestyle, I've experienced a remarkable improvement in my well-being—issues such as elevated blood pressure and joint pain, often linked to inflammation, have markedly improved. This shift in diet is not merely about adhering to medical guidance; it's about personally witnessing the significant advantages of a purer, more nutritious eating pattern.

One note on salt: While I haven't completely eliminated it from my diet like some others, I do use significantly less than I used to. My rationale for this is that I opt for salts that provide a rich array of minerals, such as Real Salt and Pink Himalayan salt.

As a Salt Substitute, you can use miso paste to replace salt in recipes. It provides both saltiness and umami. Use 1/2 to 1 teaspoon of miso paste per teaspoon of salt and adjust to taste.

As I age, I've become more attuned to how food affects my body. While I'm not flawless in my dietary choices, I strive to maintain a diet based on whole foods and am actively working to eliminate refined sugars. I compiled this cookbook as a personal resource and as a collection of recipes to share with others on a similar path to wellness.

Chapter 1: Oat-standing Wellness: Unveiling the Super Grain's Superpowers

Oats are a nutritional powerhouse, offering a wide range of health benefits. As a gluten-free whole grain, oats are packed with essential vitamins, minerals, fiber, and antioxidants, making them a valuable addition to any diet for promoting overall health and well-being.

Nutritional Value of Oats

Oats are incredibly nutritious, providing a balanced combination of carbohydrates, protein, fat, and fiber when prepared as oatmeal. A half cup (40.5 g) of dry oats contains significant amounts of essential nutrients, including manganese, phosphorus, magnesium, copper, iron, zinc, folate, and vitamins B1 (thiamine) and B5 (pantothenic acid) (U.S. Department of Agriculture, n.d.). These nutrients are crucial for various bodily functions, such as energy production, bone health, and immune support.

Health Benefits of Oats

1. **Antioxidants:** Oats are rich in antioxidants, particularly avenanthramides, which have potent anti-inflammatory properties. These antioxidants help improve blood flow by increasing the production of nitric oxide, which dilates blood vessels and reduces inflammation (Collins, 2018).

2. **Soluble Fiber:** Oats contain a type of soluble fiber called beta-glucan, which has numerous health benefits. Beta-glucan helps lower cholesterol levels by forming a gel-like substance in the gut that binds to cholesterol-rich bile acids and removes them from the body. Additionally, beta-glucan can stabilize blood sugar levels by slowing down the absorption of carbohydrates (Whitehead, Beck, Tosh, & Wolever, 2014).

3. **Heart Health:** Regular consumption of oats is associated with a reduced risk of heart disease. The beta-glucan in oats can lower LDL (bad) cholesterol levels and overall cholesterol levels, which are risk factors for cardiovascular disease. Furthermore, the antioxidants in oats contribute to heart health by protecting against oxidative stress and inflammation (Maki, Galant, Samuel, Tesser, Witchger, Ribaya-Mercado, & Blumberg, 2007).

4. **Weight Loss:** Oats promote satiety, helping you feel full longer, which can aid in weight management. The high fiber content slows digestion and increases the release of satiety hormones, reducing overall calorie intake. This makes oats an excellent addition to a weight loss or weight maintenance diet (Slavin & Green, 2007).

5. **Skin Benefits:** The antioxidants in oats, particularly avenanthramides, contribute to healthy skin. Oats have been used for centuries in skincare to soothe and moisturize the skin, reduce itching, and treat conditions like eczema. Their anti-inflammatory properties help calm irritated skin and provide relief from various skin conditions (Reynertson, Garay, Nebus, & Rodriguez, 2015).

6. **Childhood Asthma:** Some studies suggest that introducing oats into a child's diet early may reduce the risk of developing asthma. The anti-inflammatory properties of oats and their ability to support a healthy immune system may contribute to this protective effect (Nwaru, Takkinen, Niemelä, Kaila, Erkkola, Ahonen, & Kalliomäki, 2010).

In summary, oats are a versatile and nutritious food with numerous health benefits. From supporting heart health and weight management to improving skin health and potentially reducing the risk of childhood asthma, oats are a valuable addition to any diet. Incorporating oats into your daily routine can contribute to overall health and well-being.

Chapter 2: Exploring the Oat Spectrum: Oat Varieties and Basics

Types of Oats

Oats are a versatile and nutritious grain that come in various forms, each with its own processing method and culinary uses. Here's a closer look at the different oat varieties:

Quick Oats

Also known as instant oats, quick oats are the most processed form. They are pre-cooked, dried, and then rolled and pressed slightly thinner than rolled oats. Quick oats cook in just a few minutes and have a mild flavor and soft texture. They are ideal for a speedy breakfast porridge or for baking when a smooth texture is desired.

Rolled Oats

Rolled oats, or old-fashioned oats, are oat groats that have been steamed and flattened with large rollers. They take longer to cook than quick oats, typically around 10-15 minutes, and have a classic oatmeal texture and a slightly nutty taste. Rolled oats are perfect for oatmeal cookies, granola, and as a topping for baked goods.

Steel-Cut Oats

Steel-cut oats are oat groats that have been chopped into two or three pieces with steel blades. They offer a chewier texture and a more robust flavor compared to rolled and quick oats. Steel-cut oats take the longest to cook, usually about 20-30 minutes, and are excellent for a hearty breakfast bowl.

Scottish Oats

Scottish oats are stone-ground oat groats, creating a meal with a creamier texture when cooked. They are similar to steel-cut oats but are ground instead of chopped. Scottish oats cook relatively quickly and are perfect for traditional Scottish porridge.

Oat Groats

The whole oat kernel is called an oat groat. It's the least processed form of oats, with only the outer husk removed. Oat groats take the longest to cook, often over 50 minutes, and have a full, hearty texture and a deep, nutty flavor. They are ideal for stews, pilafs, and as a rice substitute in risotto.

Each type of oat is processed differently, which affects its cooking time, texture, and flavor. Quick oats are steamed and flattened to cook quickly, while rolled oats are simply steamed and rolled. Steel-cut oats are cut into pieces to preserve more of the grain's texture, and Scottish oats are ground for a unique, creamy consistency. Oat groats, being the least processed, retain the most nutrients and texture but require the longest cooking time.

Enjoy incorporating these oat varieties into your culinary creations, each bringing its unique characteristics to your dishes!

> What do oats say when they're feeling confident?
>
> I'm feeling oat-standing!

Best Practices for Storing Oats

Proper storage of oats and oatmeal is essential to maintain their freshness, flavor, and nutritional value. Here are the recommended methods:

Airtight Containers

Store your oats in airtight containers to protect them from moisture and pests. Glass or plastic containers with tight-fitting lids are ideal. This method prevents the absorption of odors and moisture, which can lead to a rancid taste and mold growth.

Cool, Dry, and Dark Place

Keep your oats in a cool, dry, and dark place, such as a pantry12. Avoid areas where they might be exposed to heat, moisture, and sunlight, as these can cause the oats to deteriorate quickly.

Freezing

For long-term storage, you can freeze your oats. This will kill any insect eggs and prevent pantry pests3. Ensure the oats are sealed properly before placing them in the freezer.

Oxygen-Free Environment

Storing oats in an oxygen-free environment can significantly extend their shelf life. You can use Mylar bags with oxygen absorbers for this purpose4.

Vacuum Sealing

Vacuum-sealing oats can also be an effective way to store them long-term. This method removes air from the container, thus protecting the oats from oxidation5.

Regular Checks

Periodically check your stored oats for any signs of spoilage, such as mold or unusual odors. If stored properly, oats can last for many years without losing their quality.

By following these storage tips, you can ensure that your oats and oatmeal stay fresh and delicious for whenever you're ready to use them in your recipes!

Chapter 3: Rolled Oats Revelry: Unrolling the Fun

Cooking Techniques and Times for Rolled Oats

Stovetop

In a saucepan, bring water or milk to a boil. Stir in rolled oats and reduce heat to a simmer. Cook for 5-7 minutes, stirring occasionally, until oats reach desired consistency.
Time: 5-7 minutes

Microwave

In a microwave-safe bowl, combine rolled oats and liquid. Microwave on high in one-minute intervals, stirring between each interval, until oats are cooked and creamy.
Time: 2-3 minutes

Baked

Preheat oven to 350°F (175°C). In a baking dish, combine rolled oats, liquid, and desired mix-ins. Bake for 20-25 minutes, or until oats are set and golden brown.
Time: 20-25 minutes

Instant Pot

Add rolled oats and liquid to the Instant Pot. Close the lid, set the valve to sealing, and cook on high pressure for 3 minutes. Quick release the pressure and stir oats before serving.
Time: 3 minutes (plus time to come to pressure)

Overnight Oats

In a jar or container, combine rolled oats, liquid, and toppings. Cover and refrigerate overnight. In the morning, stir and enjoy cold or warmed. There are recipes included in **Chapter 8: Morning Oat Magic: Rise and Shine Recipes.**

With these foolproof methods, you can effortlessly prepare perfect oatmeal using rolled oats. Experiment with different techniques to find your favorite way to enjoy this wholesome breakfast staple.

Groovy Groats: The Whole Oat Adventure

Oat Groats: The Purest Form of Oats

Oat groats are the purest and most unprocessed form of oats, with the husk removed but the bran and germ intact. These whole grains are minimally processed, preserving their natural nutritional value and wholesome qualities.

Nutty Flavor and Chewy Texture

One of the defining characteristics of oat groats is their distinct nutty flavor and satisfyingly chewy texture. When cooked, oat groats retain a pleasant firmness, offering a delightful mouthfeel that adds depth to dishes. Their natural nuttiness adds a rich, earthy taste to both sweet and savory recipes, making them a versatile ingredient in various cuisines.

Due to their hearty texture and robust flavor, oat groats are often used in pilafs, salads, soups, and hearty breakfast bowls. They provide a satisfying bite and contribute to the overall flavor profile of the dish, enhancing its depth and complexity.

Incorporating oat groats into your diet not only introduces you to the purest form of oats but also brings a wholesome and nutritious element to your meals. Whether enjoyed as a standalone dish or as part of a flavorful recipe, oat groats offer a satisfying eating experience that celebrates the natural essence of this ancient grain.

Methods of Cooking Oat Groats

Stovetop Method

1. Rinse oat groats under cold water and drain.
2. In a saucepan, combine 1 part oat groats with 3 parts water or broth.
3. Bring to a boil, then reduce heat to low and simmer, covered, for 50-60 minutes or until tender, stirring occasionally.
4. Remove from heat and let stand for a few minutes before serving.

Instant Pot Method

1. Rinse 1 cup oat groats under cold water and drain.
2. Place the rinsed oat groats in the Instant Pot.
3. Add 3 cups of water. If you like, you can also add a pinch of sea salt for flavor.
4. Secure the lid on the Instant Pot and ensure the valve is set to the "Sealing" position.
5. Select the "Manual" or "Pressure Cook" function and set the timer for 30 minutes on high pressure.
6. Once the cooking time is complete, let the pressure release naturally. This means you don't need to do anything; just let the Instant Pot sit until the pressure indicator drops, which can take an additional 15-20 minutes.
7. Once the pressure has fully released, open the lid. Stir the oat groats to check their consistency. They should be tender and slightly chewy. Fluff with a fork before serving.

Baked Method:

1. Preheat oven to 375°F (190°C).
2. Rinse oat groats under cold water and drain.
3. In a baking dish, combine 1 part oat groats with 2 parts water or broth.
4. Cover with foil and bake for 1 hour or until tender and liquid is absorbed.

Slow Cooker Method:

1. Rinse oat groats in water and drain.
2. In a slow cooker, combine 1 part oat groats with 4 parts water or broth.
3. Cook on low for 6-8 hours or on high for 3-4 hours, until tender.

Serve

Serve the oat groats hot. You can enjoy them as a savory dish with toppings like sautéed vegetable, or as a sweet breakfast cereal with fruits, nuts, and a splash of milk or a sweetener of your choice.

Adjusting Consistency: If you prefer your oat groats to be softer or thicker, you can adjust the water amount slightly or add a few more minutes to the cooking time.

Flavor Variations: Consider adding spices like cinnamon or vanilla extract before cooking for added flavor.

Storage: Leftover oat groats can be stored in an airtight container in the refrigerator for up to 5 days. Reheat them in the microwave or on the stovetop with a little extra water or milk to loosen them up.

Steel-Cut Oats: A Cut Above the Rest Cooking Techniques

Stovetop Steel-Cut Oats

Ingredients:

- 1 cup steel-cut oats
- 4 cups water or milk
- Pinch of sea salt (optional)

Instructions:

1. Bring water or milk to a boil in a medium saucepan, adding a pinch of salt if desired.
2. Stir in steel-cut oats, reduce the heat to low, and simmer for 20-30 minutes, stirring occasionally until the oats are tender and the liquid is mostly absorbed.
3. Let sit for a few minutes before serving with your favorite toppings.

Microwave Steel-Cut Oats

Ingredients:

- 1/4 cup steel-cut oats
- 1 cup water or milk
- Pinch of sea salt (optional)

Instructions:

4. Put ingredients in a large microwave-safe bowl
5. Microwave on high for 5 minutes, then stir. Continue microwaving in 1-minute increments, stirring between each, until the oats are tender and have absorbed most of the liquid (about 7-10 minutes total).
6. Let it sit for a minute to thicken.
7. Stir and add toppings of your choice.

Baked Steel-Cut Oats

Ingredients:

- 1 cup steel-cut oats
- 3 cups water or plant-based milk (such as almond, soy, or oat milk)
- 1/3 cup maple syrup or another sweetener of your choice
- 1 tsp baking powder
- 1 tsp cinnamon
- 1/2 tsp sea salt
- 1 tsp vanilla extract
- 1 cup fruit (optional, like berries, apples, or bananas)
- 1 tbsp chia seeds or ground flaxseeds (optional, for added texture and nutrition)

Instructions:

1. Preheat your oven to 350°F (175°C) and lightly grease an 8x8 inches (20x20 cm) or 2-quart (1.9 liter) baking dish or line it with parchment paper.

2. In a large bowl, combine dry ingredients

3. In another bowl, combine wet ingredients

4. Add the wet ingredients to the dry ingredients and mix well. Fold in 1 cup of fruit if using.

5. Pour the mixture into the prepared baking dish and bake for 50-60 minutes, or until the top is golden brown and the mixture is set. The oats should be tender and most of the liquid should be absorbed.

6. Let cool slightly before serving. You can enjoy it warm or at room temperature.

Additional Tips:

Toppings: After baking, top with additional fresh fruit, nuts, seeds, or a drizzle of more maple syrup if desired.

Storage: Store any leftovers in an airtight container in the refrigerator for up to 5 days. Reheat in the microwave or oven with a splash of liquid to moisten.

Customization: Add spices like nutmeg or ginger for more flavor, mix in dried fruits like raisins or chopped dates.

Instant Pot Steel-Cut Oats

- 1 cup steel-cut oats
- 3 cups water or milk
- Pinch of sea salt (optional)

Instructions:

1. Add 1 cup of steel-cut oats, 3 cups of water or milk, and a pinch of sea salt to the Instant Pot.

2. Select the "Manual" or "Pressure Cook" function and set the timer for 10 minutes on high pressure.

3. When complete, let the pressure release naturally for 10 minutes, then quick release any remaining pressure.

4. Open the lid, stir the steel-cut oats, and serve with your favorite toppings.

Slow-Cooked Steel-Cut Oats

- 1 cup steel-cut oats
- 4 cups water or milk
- Pinch of sea salt (optional)

Instructions:

1. Add ingredients to the slow cooker.
2. Set the slow cooker to low and cook for 6-8 hours, or overnight, until the oats are tender and creamy.
3. Stir the oats occasionally, if possible, especially if cooking during the day.
4. In the morning, give it a good stir and serve with your favorite toppings.

Tips for Perfect Steel-Cut Oats

Adjusting Consistency: For thicker oats, reduce the liquid slightly. For creamier oats, increase the liquid.

Flavor Enhancements: Consider adding spices like cinnamon, nutmeg, or vanilla extract during cooking.

Toppings: Fresh fruits, nuts, seeds, sweeteners like honey or maple syrup, and dairy or non-dairy milk are great additions to enhance the flavor and nutritional value of your steel-cut oats.

Enjoy your perfectly cooked steel-cut oats, a nutritious and satisfying meal to start your day!

> Why did the oat start a band?
>
> Because it wanted to be a rock-oat star!

> **Environmental Benefits:** Oats are considered an environmentally friendly crop because they require less fertilizer and pesticide use compared to other cereal grains. They also have deep root systems that help prevent soil erosion.

Chapter 4: Oat Flour: The Flourishing Oat: A Powdery Tale

To create oat flour, you can use oat groats, steel-cut oats, or rolled oats. A grain grinder is best for denser oats, while a blender or food processor is suitable for rolled oats. Process the oats until they reach a fine flour consistency, then sift to remove any larger pieces.

Oat flour is gluten-free and ideal for recipes that benefit from a moist texture, such as pancakes and cookies. You can generally replace 25-30% of wheat flour with oat flour in these recipes.

For gluten-free baking, mix oat flour with other flours like almond or rice flour and add a binding agent like xanthan gum or chia seeds to replicate gluten's elasticity.

Here's a suggested gluten-free flour blend:

- Brown Rice Flour: 25%
- White Rice Flour: 25%
- Tapioca Starch: 15%
- Potato Starch: 15%
- Xanthan Gum: 5%
- Oat Flour: 20%

Adjust the blend to suit your taste or recipe needs. Always sift the flours and starches for even distribution before baking.

Almond flour and oat flour can be combined in a 1:2 ratio for added richness and structure. Rice flour pairs well with oat flour for its light texture and neutral flavor.

Remember, oat flour isn't suitable for recipes that require gluten's structural properties, like yeast bread. Instead, consider the blend we do at our house, of equal amounts of hard red wheat, white wheat, and oat groats for a robust whole-grain option.

Making oat flour at home is simple and allows for customization in your baking. Gradually introduce whole grains into your diet by mixing them with all-purpose flour to ease the transition.

What do you call an oat that's been to space?

An astro-grainaut!

Chapter 5: The Milky Way of Oats: Dairy-Free Delights

Soak the Oats

Measure 1 cup of rolled oats and place them in a bowl. Cover the oats with water and let them soak for at least 30 minutes. Soaking helps to soften the oats and reduce the sliminess in the final milk.

Drain and Rinse

After soaking, drain the oats using a fine-mesh sieve and rinse them thoroughly under cold water. Rinsing helps to remove excess starch, which can contribute to a slimy texture.

Blend the Oats

Place the soaked and rinsed oats in a blender. Add 4 cups of cold water. Blend on high for 30-45 seconds. Avoid blending for too long, as over-blending can make the oat milk slimy.

Strain the Milk

Pour the blended mixture through a nut milk bag, fine-mesh sieve, or cheesecloth into a large bowl or pitcher. Squeeze or press the mixture to extract as much liquid as possible. This will leave you with smooth oat milk and oat pulp.

Optional Sweetening and Flavoring

If you prefer, you can add sweeteners or flavorings to your oat milk. For sweetness, add a tbsp of maple syrup, honey, or a couple of dates. For flavor, add a pinch of sea salt, a tsp of vanilla extract, or a dash of cinnamon. Blend the oat milk with these additions for a few seconds until combined.

Store the Oat Milk

Transfer the oat milk to a sealed container and store it in the refrigerator. Shake well before each use, as homemade oat milk can naturally separate. It will keep for up to 5 days. Enjoy your homemade oat milk as a dairy-free alternative in cereals, smoothies, and baking!

SmoOatth Operators: The Smoothie Symphony

Berry Oat Bliss
- 1 cup oat milk
- 1/2 cup mixed berries (strawberries, blueberries, raspberries)
- 1 ripe banana
- 1 tbsp chia seeds
- A pinch of sea salt (optional)
- Ice cubes (optional)

Tropical Oat Dream
- 1 cup oat milk
- 1/2 cup pineapple chunks
- 1/2 cup mango pieces
- 1/2 ripe banana
- 1 tbsp flaxseeds
- A dash of cinnamon

Green Oat Reviver
- 1 cup oat milk
- 1 cup spinach or kale
- 1/2 green apple, cored and sliced
- 1/2 avocado
- 1 tbsp hemp seeds
- A squeeze of fresh lemon juice

Chocolate Oat Indulgence
- 1 cup oat milk
- 1 ripe banana
- 2 tbsp cocoa powder
- 1 tbsp almond butter
- 1 tsp vanilla extract
- A pinch of sea salt (optional)

Peachy Oat Sunrise
- 1 cup oat milk
- 1 cup sliced peaches (fresh or frozen)
- 1/2 ripe banana
- 1 tbsp sunflower seeds
- A dash of nutmeg

Cinnamon Apple Pie Smoothie
- 1 cup oat milk
- 1 apple, cored and chopped
- 1/2 tsp cinnamon
- 1 tbsp rolled oats
- A pinch of sea salt (optional)
- Ice cubes (optional)

Blueberry Muffin Smoothie

- 1 cup oat milk
- 1/2 cup blueberries (fresh or frozen)
- 1 ripe banana
- 1 tbsp rolled oats
- 1/2 tsp vanilla extract

Carrot Cake Smoothie

- 1 cup oat milk
- 1/2 cup chopped carrots
- 1 ripe banana
- 1/4 tsp ground ginger
- 1/4 tsp nutmeg
- 1 tbsp walnuts

Pumpkin Spice Smoothie

- 1 cup oat milk
- 1/2 cup pumpkin puree
- 1 ripe banana
- 1/4 tsp pumpkin pie spice
- 1 tbsp pumpkin seeds

Golden Turmeric Smoothie

- 1 cup oat milk
- 1 ripe banana
- 1/2 tsp turmeric powder
- 1/4 tsp cinnamon
- 1 tbsp almonds
- A dash of black pepper (to enhance turmeric absorption)

Zesty Mango Lime Smoothie

- 1 cup oat milk
- 1 cup mango chunks (fresh or frozen)
- Juice of 1 lime (or 2 tbsp lime juice)
- 1 tbsp hemp seeds
- A few mint leaves

Raspberry Lemonade Smoothie

- 1 cup oat milk
- 1/2 cup raspberries (fresh or frozen)
- Juicc of 1 lemon (or 2 tbsp lemon juice)
- 1 ripe banana
- 1 tbsp flaxseeds

Feel free to adjust the ingredients to your taste and add more oat milk if you prefer a thinner consistency. Enjoy your delicious and nutritious smoothies!

Oat Milk Magic: Turning Liquid Oats into Creamy Yogurt

Making yogurt from oat milk at home is a simple process that requires only a few ingredients and some patience. Here are the step-by-step instructions:

Ingredients:

- 4 cups oat milk (homemade or store-bought, unsweetened)
- 2 tbsp plain, unsweetened yogurt with live cultures, 2 tbsp plain, unsweetened yogurt with live cultures, a yogurt starter culture or capsules with a Probiotic Blend of about 50 billion CFU

- 2 tbsp cornstarch or agar-agar powder (optional, for thickening)
- 1-2 tbsp maple syrup or sugar (optional, to feed the cultures)

Instructions:

Heat the Oat Milk

1. Pour 4 cups of oat milk into a medium saucepan. If you prefer a thicker yogurt, whisk in 2 tbsp of cornstarch or agar-agar powder until fully dissolved.
2. Heat the oat milk over medium heat until it reaches 180°F (82°C), stirring occasionally. This helps to sterilize the milk and activate the thickener if used. Do not let it boil.

Cool the Oat Milk

3. Remove the saucepan from heat and let the oat milk cool to around 110°F (43°C). This is the optimal temperature for the live cultures to thrive.
4. Inoculate with Cultures
5. Once the oat milk has cooled to the right temperature, add 2 tbsp of plain, unsweetened yogurt with live cultures or the yogurt starter culture to the milk. If you like, add 1-2 tbsp of maple syrup or sugar to feed the cultures and promote fermentation. Stir gently to combine.

Yogurt Incubation Guide

6. Transfer the yogurt mixture into a clean glass or ceramic container.
7. Secure the container with a lid or a clean cloth.
8. Place the container in a warm environment to maintain a steady temperature of around 110°F (43°C).
9. The incubation period should last between 8-12 hours.

Suitable devices for maintaining the temperature include:

Yogurt Maker: Follow the manufacturer's instructions.
Oven: Keep the light on to generate a mild heat.
Slow Cooker: Use the "keep warm" setting.
Warm Spot: Find a cozy area in your kitchen that retains heat. I have seen people set their yogurt on the floor just in front of their refrigerator. Just check the temperature to see if this might work.
Instant Pot: Close the lid (the vent can remain in the "venting" position). Press the "Yogurt" button. Set the timer for 8-12 hours.
The Instant Pot will automatically regulate the ideal temperature for yogurt fermentation.
Air Fryer: Adjust the air fryer to a low temperature, around 110°F (43°C). If the air fryer's temperature doesn't go this low, use the lowest setting and manually turn it on and off to keep a consistent warmth.
Check:
Inspect the yogurt after 8 hours.
If the yogurt has reached a desirable thickness and tanginess, it's ready.

Or for a more pronounced tang and thicker texture, continue to ferment for up to 12 hours.
Remember, the key to perfect yogurt is maintaining the right temperature and giving it time to develop its flavor and consistency. Enjoy your homemade yogurt!

Chill and Set the Yogurt
Once the yogurt has reached your desired thickness and flavor, transfer it to the refrigerator to cool and set for at least 2 hours. This helps to further thicken the yogurt.
Serve:
After chilling, your oat milk yogurt is ready to enjoy. You can eat it plain or add your favorite toppings such as fresh fruit, granola, or a drizzle of honey.
Storage:

Store the yogurt in an airtight container in the refrigerator for up to 5-7 days. Remember to save a couple of tbsp of your homemade yogurt to use as a starter culture for your next batch.

Starter Culture: Remember to save a small amount of your homemade yogurt to use as a starter for your next batch.

Oatstanding Oat Milk Yogurt Creations

Unleash the culinary magic of your oat milk yogurt with these delightful inspirations:

Awaken with Oats: Oat Milk Yogurt Breakfast Inspirations

Berry Bliss Bowl
Swirl oat milk yogurt with a touch of vanilla extract and maple syrup.
Top with a colorful array of berries like strawberries, blueberries, and raspberries.
Sprinkle with chia seeds and a drizzle of honey for extra sweetness.

Tropical Morning Bowl
Mix oat milk yogurt with a spoonful of date sugar or agave nectar.
Add diced mango, pineapple, and kiwi for a tropical taste.
Garnish with shredded coconut and a few mint leaves.

Apple Cinnamon Delight
Combine oat milk yogurt with cinnamon and a splash of apple juice. Layer with sautéed apples and a sprinkle of granola for crunch. Finish with a dollop of almond butter and a sprinkle of nutmeg.

Peanut Butter Banana Bowl
Stir in some creamy peanut butter into your oat milk yogurt.
Slice bananas on top and add a handful of dark chocolate chips.
Top with crushed peanuts and a drizzle of caramel sauce.

Cherry Almond Sunrise
Flavor your oat milk yogurt with almond extract and a bit of honey.
Pit and halve fresh cherries to scatter on top.
Add slivered almonds and dark chocolate shavings for a decadent touch.

22

Peaches and Cream Bowl

Sweeten oat milk yogurt with honey or stevia.

Layer with sliced peaches and a sprinkle of cinnamon.

Top with a crumble of oat cookies and a splash of oat milk.

Fig and Walnut Wonder

Infuse oat milk yogurt with a hint of orange zest and a splash of vanilla.

Arrange sliced figs and a handful of walnuts on top.

Drizzle with agave nectar and a pinch of sea salt.

Mediterranean Oat Yogurt Bowl

Combine oat milk yogurt with a dash of lemon juice, and sea salt.

Add chopped cucumbers, cherry tomatoes, olives, and roasted red peppers.

Garnish with fresh dill, parsley, or mint.

Serve with warm pita bread on the side.

Southwest Oat Yogurt Breakfast Bowl

Start with a base of oat milk yogurt seasoned with taco spices.

Top with black beans, corn, diced avocado, and fresh cilantro.

Include a scoop of salsa and a sprinkle of nutritional yeast for a cheesy flavor.

Finish with a squeeze of lime for zest.

Asian-Inspired Oat Yogurt Bowl:

Mix oat milk yogurt with a bit of soy sauce, tahini, and rice vinegar.

Add shredded carrots, sliced cucumbers, and edamame beans.

Top with sesame seeds, green onions, and a drizzle of sriracha.

Pair with rice crackers or steamed rice.

Hearty Greens Oat Yogurt Bowl

Stir a spoonful of pesto into your oat milk yogurt for a herby base.

Layer on sautéed kale, spinach, or Swiss chard.

Add roasted cherry tomatoes and artichoke hearts.

Sprinkle with hemp seeds or chopped nuts for added texture.

Indian Spiced Oat Yogurt Bowl

Season oat milk yogurt with garam masala, turmeric, and cumin. Incorporate roasted cauliflower, chickpeas, and sweet potatoes. Garnish with fresh coriander and a dollop of mango chutney.
Serve with a piece of naan or roti.

Savory Oat Yogurt Parfait Layer oat milk yogurt with diced tomatoes, cucumbers, olives, and a sprinkle of za'atar or your favorite herbs for a Mediterranean twist.

Oat Yogurt Breakfast Tacos

Fill soft corn tortillas with oat milk yogurt, scrambled tofu, black beans, avocado, and a drizzle of hot sauce for a zesty start.

Oat Yogurt Quiche

Blend oat milk yogurt with chickpea flour and nutritional yeast to create a quiche filling. Pour into a crust and bake until set.

Oat Yogurt and Herb Dip

Mix oat milk yogurt with fresh dill, chives, and garlic for a tangy dip. Serve with roasted baby potatoes or a selection of raw vegetables.

Oat Yogurt Avocado Toast

Spread oat milk yogurt on toasted bread, top with sliced avocado, a squeeze of lemon, and a pinch of chili flakes for a creamy and spicy treat.

Oat Yogurt Breakfast Bruschetta

Top toasted bread with a smear of oat milk yogurt, diced tomatoes, basil, and a balsamic reduction for an Italian-inspired dish.

Savory Oat Yogurt Smoothie Bowl

Blend oat milk yogurt with spinach, avocado, and a touch of garlic. Top with roasted chickpeas and a sprinkle of paprika.

Dip Dynamos: Unleash the Creamy Crusaders!

Sandwich Saviors
Elevate your bread-bound creations with spreads that spread joy and flavor in equal measure.

Wrap Wizards
Cast a delicious spell on your wraps with a swirl of these creamy concoctions.

Herbed Garlic & Chive Spread
Mix oat milk yogurt with minced garlic, chopped chives, dill, and a touch of lemon juice for a fresh and tangy spread.

Spicy Chipotle Dip
Blend oat milk yogurt with chipotle peppers in adobo sauce, smoked paprika, and cumin for a smoky and spicy kick.

Cool Cucumber Dill Dip
Combine grated cucumber with oat milk yogurt, fresh dill, and a hint of garlic for a cool and refreshing dip.

Roasted Red Pepper Hummus
Process roasted red peppers, roasted garlic, chickpeas, oat milk yogurt, tahini, and a splash of lemon juice for a creamy and vibrant hummus.

Curried Yogurt Spread
Stir curry powder, turmeric, and cilantro into oat milk yogurt for a spread with a warm and exotic flavor profile.

Sundried Tomato & Basil Pesto
Blend sundried tomatoes, fresh basil, oat milk yogurt, and pine nuts for a tangy pesto that's perfect on sandwiches.

Zesty Avocado Lime Spread
Mash avocado with oat milk yogurt, lime zest, and juice for a zesty and creamy spread ideal for wraps.

Sweet and Spicy Mango Chutney
Mix oat milk yogurt with mango chutney, a dash of cayenne pepper, and chopped cilantro for a sweet yet spicy dip.

Tzatziki-Inspired Dip
Grate cucumber and mix with oat milk yogurt, minced garlic, and mint, for a Greek-inspired tzatziki.

Balsamic Fig Compote Spread
Simmer figs with balsamic vinegar until thickened, then blend with oat milk yogurt for a sweet and tangy spread.

Feel free to experiment and create blends that cater to your taste buds.

Chill Factor: Fro-Yo Fantasies & Popsicle Dreams

Berry Swirl Frozen Yogurt

Ingredients:

- 2 cups oat milk yogurt
- 1 cup mixed berries (strawberries, blueberries, raspberries)
- 1/4 cup honey, date syrup or maple syrup
- 1 tsp vanilla extract

Instructions:

1. Puree the berries with sweetener and vanilla until smooth.
2. Swirl the berry puree into the oat milk yogurt, creating a marbled effect.
3. Pour the mixture into a freezer-safe container and freeze until solid, stirring every 30 minutes for the first 2 hours to maintain a creamy texture.

Mango Pineapple Popsicles

Ingredients:

- 2 cups oat milk yogurt
- 1 cup mango, chopped
- 1 cup pineapple, chopped
- 2 tbsp agave syrup

Instructions:

1. Blend the mango, pineapple, and agave syrup until smooth.
2. Layer the fruit puree and oat milk yogurt in popsicle molds.
3. Insert popsicle sticks and freeze until solid, about 4-6 hours.

Chocolate Peanut Butter Froyo Bites

Ingredients:

- 2 cups oat milk yogurt
- 1/4 cup cocoa powder
- 1/4 cup peanut butter, melted
- 2 tbsp date sugar

Instructions:

1. Mix the oat milk yogurt with cocoa powder and date sugar.
2. Spoon a layer of the yogurt mixture into silicone muffin cups.
3. Drizzle with melted peanut butter and use a toothpick to create swirls.
4. Freeze until firm, then pop out and enjoy!

Cinnamon Apple Popsicles

Ingredients:

- 2 cups oat milk yogurt
- 1 cup unsweetened applesauce
- 1 tsp cinnamon
- 2 tbsp maple syrup

Instructions:

1. Mix all ingredients until well combined.
2. Pour the mixture into popsicle molds and freeze until solid.

Raspberry Choco-Chip Frozen Yogurt

Ingredients:

- 2 cups oat milk yogurt
- 1 cup raspberries
- 1/4 cup chocolate chips
- 2 tbsp honey

Instructions:

1. Gently fold raspberries and chocolate chips into the oat milk yogurt.
2. Sweeten with honey to taste.
3. Freeze in a container, stirring occasionally, until desired consistency is reached.

Tropical Twist Frozen Yogurt Bars

Ingredients:

- 2 cups oat milk yogurt
- 1/2 cup coconut flakes
- 1/2 cup diced kiwi
- 1/2 cup diced mango
- 1/4 cup honey (or agave syrup)

Instructions:

1. Spread the oat milk yogurt in a thin layer on a baking sheet lined with parchment paper.
2. Sprinkle with coconut flakes, kiwi, and mango.
3. Drizzle with honey and freeze until solid. Break into bars and serve.

These recipes are just a starting point. Feel free to get creative with your flavors and mix-ins to create your own frozen masterpieces. Enjoy your homemade frozen treats!

Dressed to Impress: Fashioning Yogurt Dressings with a Twist

Creamy Herb Dressing

Ingredients:

- 1 cup oat milk yogurt
- 1/4 cup chopped fresh herbs (parsley, dill, chives) (1 tbsp dry)
- 2 tbsp lemon juice
- 1 garlic clove, minced
- Salt and pepper to taste (optional)

Instructions:

1. Combine all ingredients in a bowl.
2. Whisk until smooth and well combined.
3. Taste and adjust seasoning as needed.

Tangy Mustard Vinaigrette

Ingredients:

- 1 cup oat milk yogurt
- 2 tbsp Dijon mustard
- 2 tbsp apple cider vinegar
- 1 tbsp maple syrup (honey, agave syrup, date syrup, or brown rice syrup)
- Salt and pepper to taste (optional)

Instructions:

1. In a bowl, whisk all ingredients until the dressing is smooth and creamy.
2. Season with salt and pepper if desired.

Zesty Avocado Lime Dressing

Ingredients:

- 1 ripe avocado
- 1 cup oat milk yogurt
- Juice of 1 lime (2 tbsp juice)
- 1/2 tsp cumin
- Salt to taste (optional)

Instructions:

1. Blend the avocado, oat milk yogurt, lime juice, and cumin until smooth.
2. Add a little water if needed to reach the desired consistency.
3. Season with salt if you wish.

Sweet and Spicy Mango Dressing

Ingredients:

- 1 cup oat milk yogurt
- 1/2 ripe mango, peeled and chopped (1/2 cup)
- 1 tbsp lime juice
- 1/2 tsp chili powder
- Salt to taste (optional)

Instructions:

1. Puree the mango, oat milk yogurt, lime juice, and chili powder until smooth.
2. Taste and add salt if needed.
3. If the dressing is too thick, thin it with a little water.

Balsamic Beet Dressing

Ingredients:

- 1 cup oat milk yogurt
- 1/2 cup roasted beets, chopped
- 2 tbsp balsamic vinegar
- Salt and pepper to taste (optional)

Instructions:

1. Blend the oat milk yogurt, beets, and balsamic vinegar until smooth.
2. Season with salt and pepper as desired.
3. Add water to adjust the consistency if necessary.

These dressings are versatile and can be adjusted to your taste. They're perfect for drizzling over fresh greens, grain bowls, or even as a dip for vegetables. Enjoy your healthy and flavorful salads!

Embrace these ideas and let your culinary creativity soar with the versatility of oat milk yogurt!

> What did oatmeal say to oat milk?
>
> You complete me!

Oat Milk Delight: A Dairy-Free Cottage Cheese Alternative

Craft your own dairy-free cottage cheese alternative with this simple recipe using oat milk. Perfect for those seeking a plant-based option, this 'Oat Milk Delight' offers a creamy texture and a versatile flavor that pairs well with a variety of dishes. Enjoy the healthful benefits without compromising on taste!

Ingredients:

- 4 cups of unsweetened oat milk
- 2 tbsp of lemon juice or vinegar
- 1 tsp of Miso (or sea salt)

Instructions:

1. **Heat the Oat Milk:** Pour the oat milk into a large pot and slowly heat it on the stove. You want to bring it to a gentle simmer, not a boil. Aim for around 200°F (93°C), just before it starts to boil.
2. **Add Acid:** Once the oat milk is hot, add the lemon juice or vinegar. This will cause the oat milk to curdle and separate into curds and whey.
3. **Let it Curdle:** Stir the mixture gently and let it sit for 10-15 minutes off the heat. You should see the curds (solid

4. parts) separate from the whey (liquid).
5. **Strain the Curds:** Line a colander with a cheesecloth or a clean, thin dish towel. Pour the mixture into the colander to separate the curds from the whey.
6. **Season:** Sprinkle the curds with salt and any other seasonings you might like.
7. **Press the Curds:** Gather the corners of the cheesecloth and gently squeeze to remove excess whey. You can press it under a weight for a firmer texture.
8. **Chill:** Place the curds in the refrigerator to chill and firm up a bit before using.

Remember, this will not be exactly like traditional cottage cheese, but it can be a tasty plant-based alternative. Enjoy your homemade oat milk cottage cheese!

Oat Milk Cottage Cheese Salad

Ingredients:

Mixed greens, cherry tomatoes, cucumber, red onion, homemade oat milk cottage cheese.

Instructions: Toss the greens, vegetables, and cottage cheese in a bowl. Drizzle with dressing and serve fresh.

Honey Mustard Dressing

Ingredients:

- 2 tbsp of mustard (Dijon or yellow)
- 1 tbsp of honey (or maple syrup)
- 2 tbsp of apple cider vinegar
- 1/4 cup of water
- Salt and pepper to taste

1. **Combine Dressing Ingredients:** In a small bowl, whisk together the mustard, honey, apple cider vinegar, and water until well blended.
2. **Season:** Add salt and pepper to taste, adjusting the seasoning as needed.
3. **Adjust Consistency:** If the dressing is too thick, add a little more water until you reach the desired consistency.
4. **Serve:** Drizzle over your cottage cheese salad just before serving.

Pepper Boats: Sailing on a Sea of Quinoa

Ingredients:

- 4 large bell peppers, any color
- 2 cups cooked quinoa or rice
- 1 cup black beans, drained and rinsed
- 1 1/2 cup corn kernels, fresh or frozen
- 1 cup homemade oat milk cottage cheese
- 1 tsp cumin
- 1 tsp paprika
- 1 tsp garlic powder
- Salt and pepper to taste
- 1/2 cup marinara sauce (optional)

Instructions:

1. **Preheat Oven:** Preheat your oven to 375°F (190°C).
2. **Prepare Bell Peppers:** Cut the tops off the bell peppers and remove the seeds and membranes. If they don't stand upright, you can slice a small portion off the bottom to level them.
3. **Mix Filling:** In a bowl, combine the cooked quinoa or rice, black beans, corn, homemade oat milk cottage cheese, cumin, paprika, garlic powder, salt, and pepper.

4. **Stuff Peppers:** Fill each bell pepper with the quinoa mixture, pressing down gently to pack the filling.
5. **Add Sauce:** If using, spoon a bit of marinara sauce over the top of each stuffed pepper.
6. **Bake:** Place the stuffed peppers in a baking dish and bake in the preheated oven for about 25-30 minutes, or until the peppers are tender and the filling is heated through.
7. **Serve:** Remove from the oven, let cool for a few minutes before serving.

Layered Bliss: Oatmeal Overture Lasagna

Ingredients:

- 9-12 lasagna noodles
- 2 cups homemade oat milk cottage cheese
- 2 cups marinara sauce
- 2 cups fresh spinach, chopped
- 1 cup mushrooms, sliced
- 1/2 cup nutritional yeast
- 1 tsp dried oregano
- 1 tsp dried basil
- Salt and pepper to taste
- Optional – add some meat alternative (hamburger, pepperoni or sausage)

Instructions:

1. **Preheat Oven:** Preheat your oven to 350°F (175°C).
2. Prepare Noodles: Cook the lasagna noodles according to package instructions until al dente. Drain and set aside.
3. **Sauté Vegetables:** In a pan over medium heat, sauté the mushrooms and spinach until the spinach is wilted and the mushrooms are soft. Season with salt and pepper.
4. **Assemble Lasagna:** Spread a thin layer of marinara sauce on the bottom of a baking dish. Place a layer of noodles over the sauce. Spread a layer of the homemade oat milk cottage cheese over the noodles, followed by the sautéed vegetables, and sprinkle with nutritional yeast, oregano, and basil. Repeat the layers until all ingredients are used, finishing with a layer of sauce and nutritional yeast on top.
5. **Bake:** Cover with foil and bake for 25 minutes. Then, remove the foil and bake for an additional 15 minutes, or until the top is golden and bubbly.
6. **Cool and Serve:** Let the lasagna cool for 10-15 minutes before slicing. This helps the layers set and makes it easier to serve.

Enjoy your hearty and healthy Lasagna!

Oat of This World: Homemade Cream Cheese

Ingredients:

1 cup homemade oat milk

1 block extra-firm tofu

2 tbsp lemon juice or vinegar for tanginess

- Thickener: choose from: 1/4 tsp xanthan gum, 1 tsp Agar-agar powder, 2 tsp corn starch, 2 tsp arrowroot powder, 1 tsp carrageenan
- A pinch of nutritional yeast (optional)
- Salt to taste

Instructions:

Prepare the oat milk: Blend ¼ cup of oats with ½ cup water until smooth, then strain through a nut milk bag or cheesecloth to obtain creamy oat milk.

Blend the tofu and oat milk: Combine the extra-firm tofu and homemade oat milk in a blender until smooth.

Add acidity: Incorporate the lemon juice/vinegar into the mixture in the blender for a tangy flavor.

Thicken: In a saucepan, gently heat the mixture and add thickening powder of choice. Stir continuously until the powder is fully dissolved and the mixture thickens.

Season: Add salt to enhance the flavor, adjusting according to your preference.

Set the cream cheese: Pour the mixture into a mold or container and let it cool. Refrigerate for a few hours until it sets and achieves a firm, spreadable consistency.

Omitting the thickener:
Instructions: Follow the recipe as written, but after adding the lemon juice/vinegar, strain the mixture through cheesecloth or a fine-mesh sieve. This will separate the thicker curds from the whey (liquid).
Thicken Naturally: Refrigerate the strained mixture for several hours. The natural acidity and cold temperature will help the mixture thicken and achieve a spreadable consistency. You may need to chill it overnight for optimal results.

Flavor variations: You can create different flavors by adding herbs, spices, or sweeteners to the blend.

Storage: Store the cream cheese in an airtight container in the refrigerator.

The Cream of the Crop: Oatstanding Cream Cheese Twists

Herb-Infused Cream Cheese
Add a mix of finely chopped herbs such as chives, dill, and parsley for a fresh, garden-inspired flavor.

Sweet and Fruity Cream Cheese
Blend in fresh berries or a swirl of fruit jam for a sweet twist that's perfect for breakfast or dessert spreads.

Garlic and Onion Cream Cheese
Incorporate roasted garlic and minced green onions for a savory and aromatic spread that pairs well with crackers and bread.

Spicy Jalapeño Cream Cheese
Mix in diced jalapeños and a dash of chili powder for a spicy kick that will liven up any dish.

Smoky Chipotle Cream Cheese
Add chipotle peppers in adobo sauce for a smoky, spicy flavor that's great for wraps and sandwiches.

Sun-Dried Tomato and Basil Cream Cheese
Stir in chopped sun-dried tomatoes and basil for a Mediterranean flair.

Maple and Cinnamon Cream Cheese
Sweeten with a bit of maple syrup and a sprinkle of cinnamon for a cozy, comforting spread.

Nutty Cream Cheese
Fold in finely ground walnuts or pecans for a nutty texture and rich flavor.

Za'atar Cream Cheese
Blend in za'atar spice mix for a Middle Eastern touch that's delicious on pita bread or bagels.

Chocolate Cream Cheese
For a decadent treat, mix in cocoa powder and a sweetener of your choice to create a chocolatey dessert spread.

Enjoy your homemade cream cheese with your favorite dishes or as a spread on bagels and toast!

Feel free to experiment with these ideas or come up with your own unique combinations to suit your taste preferences.

Oat Milk Tofu

Ingredients:

- 1 cup oat milk
- 1/2 tsp thickener of choice (agar powder, cornstarch, arrowroot, tapioca starch, or xanthan gum)
- 1/2 tsp lemon juice or vinegar
- Optional add-ins: nutritional yeast, turmeric, garlic powder, salt, and pepper

Instructions:

1. **Heat the Oat Milk:** Pour the oat milk into a saucepan and bring it to a gentle simmer over medium heat.
2. **Add Thickener:** dissolve in a small amount of cold oat milk and then add to the simmering oat milk, stirring constantly until it thickens. If using xanthan gum: add directly to the blender with the oat milk and blend until smooth and thickened.
3. **Coagulate the Milk:** Add the lemon juice or vinegar and stir gently. The mixture will start to curdle and form tofu-like curds.
4. **Strain the Curds:** Pour the mixture through a fine mesh strainer lined with cheesecloth or a nut milk bag. Gather the edges of the cloth and squeeze out as much liquid as possible.
5. **Press the Tofu:** Place the curds in a container and press them under a weight for about 15-20 minutes to remove excess moisture.
6. **Season:** Mix in your optional add-ins.

Suggestions on What to Do with Your Oat Milk Tofu:

- **Marinated Baked Tofu Cubes:** Marinade using soy sauce, minced garlic, grated ginger, and a touch of maple syrup. Bake at 375°F (190°C) for 25-30 minutes.
- **Tofu Scramble:** Crumble tofu and sautéing it with vegetables like bell peppers, onions, and spinach. Season with turmeric, black salt, and nutritional yeast.
- **Tofu Ricotta:** Blend tofu with fresh basil, garlic, and lemon juice to make a creamy ricotta-style spread. Use it in lasagna, stuffed pasta shells, or as a dip.
- **Tofu Smoothie Bowl:** Blend tofu with frozen berries, banana, and a splash of oat milk, and top with granola, nuts, and fresh fruit.
- **Tofu Stir-Fry:** Slice tofu into thin strips and stir-fry with vegetables like bell peppers, snap peas, and broccoli. Add a flavorful sauce made from soy sauce, ginger, and garlic.

Oats-So-Cheesy: Dairy-Free Delights for the Conscious Cook

Alfred-Oat's Creamy Concoction: The Dairy-Free Delight

Ingredients:

- 2 cups oat milk
- 4 tbsp oat flour
- 4 cloves garlic, minced
- Salt and pepper to taste
- Fresh parsley, chopped (for garnish)
- 1/4 cup nutritional yeast (optional, for a cheesy flavor)
- (as a butter substitute for richness) 1/2 cup of one of the following: (unsweetened applesauce, Mashed Banana, Pumpkin Puree, Mashed Avocado, Tofu, Yogurt or Cream Cheese)

Instructions:

1. **Prepare the garlic:** In a non-stick saucepan, add a little water or vegetable broth and sauté the minced garlic until fragrant.
2. **Make the roux:** Sprinkle the flour over the garlic and continue to sauté for a minute, adding more water or vegetable broth as needed to keep it from sticking.
3. **Combine:** Gradually pour in the oat milk, whisking constantly to prevent lumps.
4. **Thicken the sauce:** Continue to cook and stir until the sauce thickens. If using, stir in the nutritional yeast for a cheesy flavor.
5. **Add butter substitute:** Mix in the unsweetened applesauce to add richness without the need for butter or oil.
6. **Season:** Add salt and pepper to taste.
7. **Garnish and serve:** Serve the sauce over your favorite pasta and garnish with fresh parsley.

Adjust the thickness by adding more oat milk if needed.

Smooth Operator: Creamy Oat Bliss "Cheese" Sauce

Ingredients:

- 1 cup oat milk
- 1 cup diced potatoes (or sweet potatoes)
- 1/2 cup diced carrots
- 1/4 cup nutritional yeast
- 2 tsp Miso (or sea salt)
- Juice of half a lemon (2 tbsp)
- 1 tsp garlic powder
- 1 tsp onion powder
- 1/2 tsp sweetener like maple syrup, honey, agave nectar, or brown rice syrup, (optional)
- 2-3 tbsp tapioca flour
- 1/2 cup soaked and drained raw cashews (optional but highly recommended for added creaminess)

Instructions:

1. **Prepare Vegetables**: Boil the potatoes and carrots until soft.
2. **Blend Base Ingredients**: In a blender, combine the cashews, oat milk, boiled potatoes and carrots, nutritional yeast, miso (or salt), lemon juice, garlic powder, onion powder, and sweetener (if using).
3. **Incorporate Tapioca Flour**: Add the tapioca flour to the blended mixture.
4. **Blend for Consistency**: Blend until the mixture is smooth and creamy. If using a high-speed blender like a Vita-Mix, continue blending until the sauce is hot and thickened.
5. **Cook for Thickness**: If not using a high-speed blender, transfer the blended mixture to a pot. Simmer over medium heat, stirring frequently, until the sauce thickens to your desired consistency.
6. **Adjust Seasoning**: Taste the sauce and adjust the seasoning if necessary.
7. **Serve**: Serve the cheese alternative sauce warm over pasta, vegetables, or use it as a dip. This sauce is also ideal for dishes that benefit from a melty texture, such as pizzas or grilled cheese sandwiches.

Tailor this dish with flavorful add-ons such as salsa, jalapeños, chili powder, smoked paprika, roasted red peppers, or mustard. For a savory twist that departs from the classic cheesy taste, feel free to omit the nutritional yeast. Plus, this recipe is freezer-friendly for convenient future indulgence.

Oatmeal "Cheese" Powder Mix

Ingredients:

- 1 cup rolled oats
- 1/3 cup nutritional yeast (for a cheesy flavor)
- 2 tsp garlic powder
- 2 tsp onion powder
- 1/2 tsp turmeric (for color)
- 1/2 tsp smoked paprika (optional)
- Sea Salt to taste (optional)

Optional add ins:

Mustard Powder: A pinch can add depth and complexity to the cheesy flavor.

Lemon Zest: A teaspoon can provide a bright, citrusy note.

Chili Flakes: If you enjoy a bit of heat, a small amount can add a nice kick.

Dried Herbs: Such as thyme, oregano, or basil for an aromatic touch.

These additions can help tailor the mix to your specific taste preferences and add an extra layer of flavor to your dishes. Enjoy experimenting with your oatmeal "cheese" powder!

Instructions:

Grind the oats

Mix the ingredients

Blend again: For a finer consistency, blend the mixture again until it's a fine powder.

Store: Store cheese powder mix in an airtight container and store it in a cool, dry place.

Instructions to make the Cheesy Sauce:

1. 1 part Oatmeal Cheese Powder Mix
2. 2 parts water, vegetable broth, or unsweetened oat milk
3. In a medium saucepan. Gradually whisk in the water or oat milk, ensuring there are no lumps.
4. Place the saucepan over medium heat and bring the mixture to a simmer, stirring constantly.
5. Continue to cook for about 5-7 minutes, or until the sauce thickens to your desired consistency.
6. Remove the saucepan from the heat. Stir in a small amount of lemon juice until well combined. The lemon juice adds a subtle tanginess.
7. Taste the sauce and adjust the seasoning with more salt or lemon juice if needed.
8. Your oatmeal cheese sauce is now ready to be drizzled over your favorite dishes, such as pasta, vegetables, or nachos.

This cheese powder mix is perfect for sprinkling over popcorn, stirring into soups, or adding to sauces for a cheesy flavor without dairy.

The Oat Whisperer's Queso: Smooth, Rich, and Nutritious

Ingredients:

- 2 cups homemade oat milk
- 1/2 cup raw cashews (soaked for 2 hours if not using a high-speed blender)
- 1/4 cup tapioca flour (starch)
- 1/4 cup nutritional yeast
- 1 tbsp lemon juice
- 1 tsp garlic powder
- 1 tsp onion powder
- 1/2 tsp ground cumin
- 1/2 tsp chili powder
- 1/4 tsp smoked paprika (optional for a smoky flavor)
- 1/4 tsp turmeric (for color)
- Salt to taste
- 1 small jalapeño, seeded and chopped (optional for heat)
- 1/4 cup diced tomatoes (optional for texture)

Prepare the Ingredients:

1. If you haven't already, make your homemade oat milk and set aside.
2. If you're using cashews and don't have a high-speed blender, soak them in water for at least 2 hours or overnight. Drain and rinse before using.

Blend the Base:

3. In a blender, combine the oat milk, soaked cashews, tapioca starch, nutritional yeast, lemon juice, garlic powder, onion powder, ground cumin, chili powder, smoked paprika, turmeric, and salt.
4. Blend until the mixture is completely smooth.

Cook the Sauce:

5. Pour the blended mixture into a saucepan and cook over medium heat.
6. Stir constantly with a whisk to prevent clumping. The sauce will start to thicken after a few minutes.

(if you have a Vitamix, you can leave it in the blender and blend until it is cooked)

Add the Extras:

Once the sauce has thickened to a creamy consistency, add the chopped jalapeño and diced tomatoes, if using. Continue to cook for another 2-3 minutes, stirring frequently.

Adjust and Serve:

Taste the Queso sauce and adjust the seasoning if needed.

Serve warm with your favorite dishes such as nachos, tacos, or as a dip.

Chapter 6: Morning Oat Magic: Rise and Shine Recipes

Homemade Instant Oatmeal Packets

Creating your own instant oatmeal packets is a great way to enjoy a quick, nutritious breakfast while controlling the ingredients and flavors.

Basic Ingredients for Instant Oatmeal Packets

- 1/2 cup rolled oats (or quick oats for a finer texture)
- 1 tbsp almond or coconut flour (optional for creaminess)
- 1 tsp chia seeds or ground flaxseeds (optional for added nutrition)
- 1/8 tsp sea salt

Instructions to turn rolled oats into a quick oat alternative for instant oatmeal

Grind the Rolled Oats

Measure out the desired amount of rolled oats. You can use a food processor, into smaller pieces. The goal is to create a finer texture that cooks quickly.

Adjust the Consistency

Depending on your preference, you can grind the oats to a fine powder (similar to instant oats) or leave them slightly coarser (resembling quick oats). Adjust the grinding time accordingly.

Assembly Instructions:

1. In a small zip-top bag or airtight container, combine the base ingredients (rolled oats, almond or coconut powder, chia seeds or ground flaxseeds, and salt).
2. Add the flavor ingredients of your choice to the bag or container.
3. Seal and shake well to mix all ingredients.

Storage Information

1. Store the packets in a cool, dry place, such as a pantry. They will keep well for up to 3 months. If using ground flaxseeds, I recommend storing them in the freezer or adding the ground flax seeds when ready to prepare the oatmeal.
2. For longer storage, you can keep the packets in the refrigerator or freezer to maintain freshness.

Microwave Method

1. Empty the contents of one packet into a microwave-safe bowl.
2. Add 3/4 cup of water or milk (adjust based on desired thickness).
3. Microwave on high for 1-2 minutes, stirring halfway through. Let it sit for 1 minute before eating.

Stovetop Method

1. Empty the contents of one packet into a small saucepan.
2. Add 3/4 cup of water or milk (adjust based on desired thickness).
3. Bring to a boil, then reduce heat and simmer for 3-5 minutes, stirring occasionally, until the oats are tender.

No-Cook Overnight Oats:

1. Empty the contents of one packet into a jar or container.
2. Add 3/4 cup of cold water or milk.
3. Stir well, cover, and refrigerate overnight.
4. In the morning, give it a stir and enjoy cold, or microwave briefly to warm it up.

Enjoy your homemade instant oatmeal packets with a variety of delicious flavors that suit your taste!

Flavor Alternatives:

Classic Cinnamon Sugar:
- 1 tsp cinnamon
- 1 tbsp date sugar

Apple Cinnamon:
- 1 tsp cinnamon
- 2 tbsp dried apple pieces
- 1 tbsp date sugar

Maple Brown Sugar:
- 1 tbsp maple sugar or maple syrup powder
- 1 tbsp date sugar

Berry Delight:
- 2 tbsp freeze-dried berries (strawberries, blueberries, raspberries)
- 1 tsp vanilla extract powder (optional)

Banana Nut:
- 2 tbsp dried banana chips (crushed)
- 1 tbsp chopped nuts (walnuts, pecans)
- 1 tsp cinnamon

Chocolate Peanut Butter:
- 1 tbsp cocoa powder
- 1 tbsp powdered peanut butter
- 1 tsp mini chocolate chips

Peach Almond:

- 2 tbsp dried peach pieces
- 1 tbsp sliced almonds
- 1/2 tsp almond extract powder (optional)

Cranberry Orange:

- 2 tbsp dried cranberries
- 1 tsp orange zest (dried or fresh)

Pumpkin Spice:

- 1 tsp pumpkin pie spice
- 1 tbsp pumpkin puree powder (optional)
- 1 tbsp date sugar

Tropical Coconut:

- 2 tbsp dried pineapple pieces
- 1 tbsp shredded coconut
- 1 tsp vanilla extract powder (optional)

Sugar Substitutes

For those looking to reduce or eliminate sugar from their diet, here are some delightful alternatives to enhance your instant oatmeal:

- **Date Paste and Date Sugar**: Are Healthier Sweetening Options. Make date paste by blending dates and water. These serve as natural sweeteners with added fiber, vitamins, and minerals. They provide both sweetness and moisture. Use a 1:1 ratio to substitute for granulated sugar. Date sugar, derived from dried and ground dates, offers antioxidants, essential minerals, and vitamin B6. Remember that date sugar has a coarser texture and a rich caramel flavor.

- **Honey, Maple Syrup, or Agave Nectar**: Drizzle these natural liquid sweeteners into your oatmeal for a touch of sweetness. Adjust the quantity to your taste preference.

- **Stevia or Monk Fruit Sweetener**: These zero-calorie sweeteners pack a powerful punch. A small dash of stevia (be cautious to avoid bitterness) or 1 tsp of monk fruit sweetener can replace 1 tbsp of sugar.

- **Erythritol or Xylitol**: These sugar alcohols offer a sweetness similar to sugar with fewer calories and no spike in blood sugar levels. Substitute them on a 1:1 basis, keeping in mind their distinct cooling aftertaste.

- **Pureed Fruits**: Incorporate pureed bananas, applesauce, or dates for a naturally sweet twist that also boosts your meal's nutritional value.

Feel free to experiment with these sugar alternatives to find your perfect oatmeal companion. Enjoy your wholesome and tasty start to the day!

Wholesome Whirls: Creamy Smoothies with a Heart-Healthy Kick

Berry Oat Bliss Smoothie

Ingredients:

- 1/2 cup rolled oats
- 1 cup oat milk
- 1 banana
- 1/2 cup mixed berries (strawberries, blueberries, raspberries)
- 1 tbsp chia seeds
- 1 tbsp maple syrup or sweetener of choice (optional)
- A pinch of cinnamon

Instructions:

Blend the oats in a blender until they become a fine powder. Add the remaining ingredients and blend until smooth.
Enjoy immediately for a berry-licious treat!

What do you call a nervous bowl of oats?

Quaker-ing in their boots!

Green Oat Power Smoothie

Ingredients:

- 1/2 cup rolled oats
- 1 cup oat milk
- 1 ripe banana
- 1 cup spinach leaves
- 1/2 avocado
- 1 tbsp almond butter
- 1 tsp lemon juice
- Honey or agave nectar to taste

Instructions:

First, grind the oats into a powder. Add the rest of the ingredients to the blender and blend until creamy. Perfect for an energizing start to your day.

Tropical Oat Sunrise Smoothie

Ingredients:

- 1/2 cup rolled oats
- 1 cup coconut water or oat milk
- 1/2 cup mango chunks
- 1/2 cup pineapple chunks
- 1/2 banana
- 1 tbsp coconut flakes
- A squeeze of fresh lime juice

Instructions:

Blend the oats until powdered.
Combine with the tropical fruits, coconut water or oat milk, and lime juice in the blender.
Blend until smooth and garnish with coconut flakes.

Peanut Butter Oatmeal Smoothie

Ingredients:

- 1/2 cup rolled oats
- 1 cup oat milk
- 1 banana
- 2 tbsp natural peanut butter
- 1 tbsp cocoa powder
- 1 tbsp honey or a pitted date

Instructions:

Start by blending the oats into a fine powder. Add the banana, peanut butter, cocoa powder, and sweetener of choice, along with the milk.
Blend until smooth and enjoy this protein-packed smoothie.

> Ancient Origins: Oats have been cultivated for thousands of years and are one of the oldest cereal grains. They were first grown in Europe and have been a staple food in many cultures throughout history.

Spiced Apple Pie Oatmeal Smoothie

Ingredients:

- 1/2 cup rolled oats
- 1 cup oat milk
- 1 apple, cored and sliced
- 1/2 tsp ground cinnamon
- 1/4 tsp ground nutmeg
- 1/4 tsp ground ginger
- 1 tbsp maple syrup or sweetener of choice
- A pinch of sea salt

Instructions:

Grind the oats into a powder.
Add the apple, spices, sweetener, and oat milk to the blender.
Blend until smooth, then pour into a glass and sprinkle a little extra cinnamon on top for a cozy, apple pie-inspired smoothie.

Chocolate Peanut Butter Oatmeal Smoothie

Ingredients:

- 1/2 cup rolled oats
- 1 cup oat milk
- 1 ripe banana
- 2 tbsp peanut butter
- 1 tbsp cocoa powder
- 1 tbsp honey or a pitted date (optional)

Instructions:

Grind the oats into a powder. Add all the ingredients and sweetener if desired. Blend until smooth for a decadent chocolate and peanut butter treat.

Cinnamon Roll Oat Smoothie

Ingredients:

- 1/2 cup rolled oats
- 1 cup oat milk
- 1 frozen banana
- 1 tbsp almond butter
- 1/2 tsp ground cinnamon
- 1/4 tsp vanilla extract
- A pinch of sea salt (optional)
- 1 tsp maple syrup (optional)

Instructions:

Blend the oats until they become a fine powder. Add the rest of the ingredients and blend until smooth.
This smoothie tastes like a cinnamon roll in a glass!

Blueberry Muffin Oat Smoothie

Ingredients:

- 1/2 cup rolled oats
- 1 cup oat milk
- 3/4 cup fresh or frozen blueberries
- 1/2 banana
- 1/4 cup oat milk yogurt
- 1/2 tsp lemon zest
- 1 tbsp honey or sweetener of choice

Instructions:

Start by grinding the oats into a fine powder. Combine with the blueberries, banana, yogurt, lemon zest, and sweetener in the blender.
Blend until creamy for a smoothie that mimics the flavors of a blueberry muffin.

Peachy Oat Sunrise Smoothie

Ingredients:

- 1/2 cup rolled oats
- 1 cup oat milk
- 1 cup frozen peaches
- 1/2 banana
- 1/2 tsp ground ginger
- 1 tbsp honey or maple syrup (optional)

Instructions:

Blend the oats until powdered. Add the peaches, banana, ginger, and sweetener, if using, to the blender.
Blend until smooth and enjoy a refreshing peach-flavored smoothie.

Oat and Berry Antioxidant Smoothie

Ingredients:

- 1/2 cup rolled oats
- 1 cup oat milk
- 1/2 cup frozen mixed berries
- 1/2 cup beetroot, cooked and diced
- 1 tbsp flaxseeds
- 1 tsp honey or sweetener of choice

Instructions:

First, grind the oats into a fine powder. Then add the berries, beetroot, flaxseeds, and sweetener, along with the oat milk, into the blender.
Blend until smooth for an antioxidant-rich start to your day.

Oatmeal is not only a hearty addition to your breakfast or snack time but also infuses each sip with a boost of nutrition. consider adding oatmeal to the variety of smoothie recipes featured in the oat milk section for even more oat-inspired beverage delights. Oatmeal is a versatile ingredient that not only thickens your smoothies but also provides additional fiber and a satisfying fullness. Start with a small amount, such as a tbsp or two, and increase as desired to achieve your preferred consistency and taste. Enjoy discovering your perfect oat-infused blend!

Cultural Significance: Oats have cultural significance in various traditions and folklore. In some cultures, oats are associated with prosperity, fertility, and good luck. They are also used in rituals and celebrations in certain societies.

Midnight Mix-Ins: Oats That Work the Night Shift

Overnight oats are a convenient, nutritious, and versatile breakfast option that can be customized with a variety of flavors and ingredients. Here's a basic recipe for overnight oats, followed by numerous delicious variations.

Basic Overnight Oats Recipe

Ingredients:

- 1/2 cup rolled oats
- 1/2 cup oat milk
- 1/4 cup yogurt (optional for creaminess)
- 1 tbsp chia seeds (optional for added texture and nutrition)
- 1-2 tsp sweetener (honey, maple syrup, agave, or a sugar substitute)
- 1/2 tsp vanilla extract (optional)

Instructions:

1. In a jar or airtight container, combine the rolled oats, milk, yogurt (if using), chia seeds, sweetener, and vanilla extract.
2. Stir well to mix all the ingredients.
3. Cover the jar or container and refrigerate overnight (at least 4 hours).
4. In the morning, give the oats a good stir and add any desired toppings before eating.

Flavor Alternatives:

Classic Vanilla:
- Add 1/2 tsp vanilla extract.
- Top with fresh berries and a drizzle of honey.

Berry Blast:
- Add 1/4 cup mixed fresh or frozen berries.
- Stir in 1 tbsp berry jam or preserves.

Banana Nut:
- Add 1/2 a sliced banana.
- Stir in 1 tbsp chopped walnuts and 1/2 tsp cinnamon.

Chocolate Peanut Butter:
- Add 1 tbsp cocoa powder.
- Stir in 1 tbsp peanut butter and 1 tsp mini chocolate chips.

Apple Cinnamon:
- Add 1/2 an apple, chopped.
- Stir in 1/2 tsp cinnamon and 1 tbsp raisins.

Maple Pecan:
- Add 1 tbsp chopped pecans.
- Stir in 1 tbsp maple syrup.

Tropical Paradise:

- Add 1/4 cup diced pineapple and 1 tbsp shredded coconut.
- Stir in 1 tbsp chopped mango.

Pumpkin Spice:

- Add 1/4 cup pumpkin puree.
- Stir in 1/2 tsp pumpkin pie spice and 1 tbsp maple syrup.

Coconut Almond:

- Add 1/4 cup unsweetened shredded coconut.
- Stir in 1 tbsp almond butter and a handful of sliced almonds.

Strawberry Cheesecake:

- Add 1/4 cup chopped strawberries.
- Stir in 1 tbsp cream cheese and 1 tbsp graham cracker crumbs.

Peach Pie:

- Add 1/4 cup diced peaches (fresh, frozen, or canned).
- Stir in 1/2 tsp cinnamon and 1 tbsp crushed graham crackers.

Blueberry Muffin:

- Add 1/4 cup fresh or frozen blueberries.
- Stir in 1 tbsp crushed nuts (walnuts or almonds) and a pinch of nutmeg.

Cinnamon Raisin:

- Add 1 tbsp raisins.
- Stir in 1/2 tsp cinnamon and 1 tbsp chopped walnuts.

Storage Information

Overnight oats can be prepared up to 3-4 days in advance and stored in the refrigerator. This makes them an excellent option for meal prep.

Preparation Instructions:

Each variation can be prepared using the same basic method combine the ingredients in a jar or container, stir well, and refrigerate overnight. In the morning, add any desired fresh toppings before serving.

Enjoy your customized overnight oats as a quick, nutritious, and delicious breakfast!

Chapter 7: The Great Granola Adventure: The Saga of Oats, Nuts, and Fruits

Embark on the Crunchy Quest with granola, a symphony of flavors that doubles as your ally in wellness. Each spoonful is not just a delight to the taste buds but also a treasure trove of health benefits. Rich in fiber and whole grains, granola supports digestive health and satiety. Its nuts and seeds offer heart-healthy fats, while the variety of fruits adds a burst of antioxidants. Together, they create a nourishing blend that energizes your mornings and fuels your adventures. Dive into the granola goodness and let each bite take you on a journey towards a healthier, happier you.

Basic Granola Recipe

Ingredients:

3 cups rolled oats
1/2 to 3/4 cup chopped nuts (such as: almonds, walnuts, pecans)
1/2 to 3/4 cup mixed seeds (pumpkin, sunflower, sesame)
1/3 cup shredded coconut (optional)
1/4 cup honey or maple syrup
1/4 cup pureed (applesauce, banana, or pumpkin)
1 tsp vanilla extract
1/2 tsp sea salt
A pinch of nutmeg (optional)
1 tsp cinnamon (optional)

Instructions:

1. Preheat your oven to 350°F (175°C).
2. In a large mixing bowl, combine the oats, nuts, seeds, coconut (if using), salt, and cinnamon.
3. In a small bowl, whisk together the honey or maple syrup, applesauce, and vanilla extract.
4. Pour the wet ingredients over the dry ingredients and stir until everything is well coated.
5. Spread the mixture evenly on a baking sheet lined with parchment paper.
6. Bake for 20-25 minutes, stirring halfway through, until the granola is lightly toasted.
7. Remove from the oven and let it cool. Stir in the chopped dried fruits.
8. Store the cooled granola in an airtight container at room temperature. *The pureed fruit adds natural sweetness and helps to bind the granola, creating clusters without the need for oil.*

Flavor Varieties and Add-Ins:

Nuts and Seeds:

- Sliced almonds
- Chopped walnuts
- Pecans
- Pumpkin seeds
- Sunflower seeds
- Flaxseeds
- Chia seeds

Dried Fruits:

- Raisins
- Dried cranberries
- Dried apricots (chopped)
- Dried cherries
- Dried blueberries
- Dried apples (chopped)
- Dried mango (chopped)

Sweeteners and Flavorings:

- Maple syrup
- Agave nectar
- Date sugar
- Molasses
- Vanilla extract
- Almond extract
- Maple extract
- Cinnamon
- Nutmeg
- Pumpkin pie spice
- Cocoa powder

Crunchy Add-Ins:

- Rice cereal
- Quinoa flakes
- Buckwheat groats
- Coconut flakes
- Banana chips

Chocolate and Treats:

- Mini chocolate chips
- White chocolate chips
- Dark chocolate chunks
- Peanut butter chips
- Butterscotch chips
- Shredded coconut

Granola Varieties

Cranberry Almond Granola:

- Add 1/2 cup dried cranberries and 1/2 cup sliced almonds to the basic recipe.
- Add 1 tsp almond extract for extra flavor.

Chocolate Coconut Granola:

- Add 1/2 cup mini chocolate chips and 1/2 cup shredded coconut to the basic recipe.
- Add 2 tbsp cocoa powder to the dry ingredients.

Maple Pecan Granola:

Replace honey with maple syrup in the basic recipe.

- Add 1/2 cup chopped pecans and 1 tsp maple extract.

Tropical Granola:
- Add 1/2 cup dried mango pieces, 1/2 cup shredded coconut, and 1/2 cup chopped dried pineapple.
- Add 1 tsp coconut extract for extra flavor.

Apple Cinnamon Granola:
- Add 1/2 cup chopped dried apples and 1 tsp cinnamon to the basic recipe.
- Add 1/4 cup chopped walnuts for extra crunch.

Pumpkin Spice Granola:
- Add 1 tsp pumpkin pie spice and 1/2 cup pumpkin seeds to the basic recipe.
- Replace honey with molasses for a richer flavor.

Peanut Butter Granola:
- Add 1/2 cup peanut butter to the wet ingredients.
- Add 1/2 cup chopped peanuts and 1/2 cup mini chocolate chips.

Storage Information
Store the granola in an airtight container at room temperature for up to 2 weeks. Or freeze it for up to 3 months.

Your homemade granola can be used in a variety of delicious recipes. Here are a few ideas:

Yogurt Parfait: Layer granola with yogurt and fresh fruit for a quick and healthy breakfast or snack.

Smoothie Bowl Topping: Sprinkle granola on top of your favorite smoothie bowl for added crunch and nutrition.

Granola Bars: Mix granola with some nut butter and honey, press into a pan, and refrigerate to make homemade granola bars.

Baked Goods: Add granola to muffin or pancake batter for extra texture and flavor.

Salad Topping: Use granola as a crunchy topping for salads, especially those with fruit or a sweet vinaigrette.

Ice Cream Topping: Sprinkle granola over ice cream or frozen yogurt for a delightful crunch.

Trail Mix: Combine granola with dried fruits, nuts, and chocolate chips for a tasty trail mix.

Bar None: Crafting the Perfect Granola Bar

Basic Granola Bar: Honey Almond Delight

Ingredients:

- 2 cups rolled oats
- 1/2 cup honey
- 1/2 cup almond butter
- 1/2 cup chopped almonds
- 1 tsp vanilla extract
- 1/4 tsp sea salt
- Optional: 1/4 cup dried cranberries

Instructions:

1. Preheat your oven to 350°F (175°C) and line an 8x8-inch baking dish with parchment paper.
2. In a large bowl, mix the oats, chopped almonds, and salt.
3. In a microwave-safe bowl, warm the honey and almond butter until they are easy to stir.
4. Stir in the vanilla extract.
5. Pour the wet ingredients into the dry ingredients and mix until well combined.
6. Press the mixture firmly into the prepared baking dish.
7. Bake for 20-25 minutes until the edges are golden brown.
8. Let cool completely before cutting into bars.

Basic Granola Bar: Maple Seed Crunch

Ingredients:

- 2 cups rolled oats
- 1/2 cup maple syrup
- 1/2 cup nut butter (sunflower seed, almond, peanut butter)
- 1/2 cup mixed seeds (pumpkin, sunflower, chia)
- 1 tsp cinnamon
- 1/4 tsp sea salt
- Optional: 1/4 cup dried fruit, chopped

Instructions:

1. Preheat your oven to 350°F (175°C) and line an 9x9 inch (23x23 cm) baking dish with parchment paper.
2. In a large bowl, mix the oats, mixed seeds, cinnamon, and salt.
3. In a microwave-safe bowl, warm the maple syrup and nut butter until they are easy to stir.
4. Pour the wet ingredients into the dry ingredients and mix until well combined.

5. Press the mixture firmly into the prepared baking dish.
6. Bake for 20-25 minutes until the edges are golden brown.
7. Let cool completely before cutting into bars.

Flavor Variations and Add-Ins

Nuts and Seeds:
- Sliced almonds
- Chopped walnuts
- Pecans
- Pumpkin seeds
- Sunflower seeds
- Flaxseeds
- Chia seeds

Dried Fruits:
- Raisins
- Dried cranberries
- Dried apricots (chopped)
- Dried cherries
- Dried blueberries
- Dried apples (chopped)
- Dried mango (chopped)

Sweeteners and Flavorings:
- Date sugar
- Molasses
- Vanilla extract
- Almond extract
- Maple extract

- Cinnamon
- Nutmeg
- Pumpkin pie spice
- Cocoa powder

Crunchy Add-Ins:
- Rice cereal
- Quinoa flakes
- Buckwheat groats
- Shredded coconut
- Banana chips

Chocolate and Treats:
- Mini chocolate chips
- White chocolate chips
- Dark chocolate chunks
- Peanut butter chips
- Butterscotch chips
- Shredded coconut

Granola Bar Varieties

Cranberry Almond Bars:
- Add 1/4 cup dried cranberries and 1/4 cup sliced almonds to the basic recipe.
- Add 1 tsp almond extract for extra flavor.

Chocolate Coconut Bars:
- Add 1/4 cup mini chocolate chips and 1/4 cup shredded coconut to the basic recipe.
- Add 2 tbsp cocoa powder to the dry ingredients.

Maple Pecan Bars:
- Replace honey with maple syrup in the basic recipe.
- Add 1/4 cup chopped pecans and 1 tsp maple extract.

Tropical Paradise Bars:
- Add 1/4 cup dried mango pieces, 1/4 cup shredded coconut, and 1/4 cup chopped dried pineapple.
- Add 1 tsp coconut extract for extra flavor.

Apple Cinnamon Bars:
- Add 1/4 cup chopped dried apples and 1 tsp cinnamon to the basic recipe.
- Add 1/4 cup chopped walnuts for extra crunch.

Pumpkin Spice Bars:
- Add 1 tsp pumpkin pie spice and 1/4 cup pumpkin seeds to the basic recipe.
- Replace honey with molasses for a richer flavor.

Peanut Butter Chocolate Bars:
- Add 1/4 cup mini chocolate chips to the basic recipe.
- Use peanut butter as the nut butter in the basic recipe.

Storage Information
- Store the granola bars in an airtight container at room temperature for up to 1 week.
- For longer storage, keep the bars in the refrigerator for up to 2 weeks or freeze them for up to 3 months.

Oat Bran Craze: In the 1980s, oat bran became a dietary sensation after studies suggested that it could help lower cholesterol levels. This led to a surge in oat bran consumption and the creation of various oat bran products, including cereals and muffins.

Chapter 8: The Oat Cuisine: Elegant Entrees from the Humble Grain

Oatstanding Entrees: Main Event Dishes

Step into the world of oat cuisine, where this versatile grain takes center stage in an array of main dishes that will tantalize your taste buds and nourish your soul. Gone are the days when oats were confined to the breakfast bowl; now, they're the star of the show, bringing heartiness and health to your dinner table. From the rustic charm of risottos to the robust flavors of stews, these oat-based entrees are here to revolutionize your mealtime routine. So, tie on your apron, and let's get cooking with oats like you've never seen them before!

Savory Oat Groats Pilaf

Ingredients:

- 1 cup oat groats
- 2 cups vegetable broth
- 1 onion, finely chopped
- 2 cloves garlic, minced
- 1 carrot, diced
- 1 bell pepper, diced
- 1 cup peas (fresh or frozen)
- 1 tsp smoked paprika
- 1 tsp thyme
- Miso (or sea salt) and pepper to taste
- Fresh parsley for garnish

Instructions:

1. Rinse the oat groats and soak them in water for 4 hours or overnight.
2. Drain the oat groats and set aside.
3. In a large pot, sauté the onion and garlic over medium heat until softened (use water or vegetable broth to avoid oil).
4. Add the carrot and bell pepper, cooking until tender.
5. Stir in the oat groats, vegetable broth, smoked paprika, thyme, salt, and pepper.
6. Bring to a boil, then reduce heat and simmer, covered, for about 30-35 minutes until the oat groats are tender and have absorbed the liquid.

7. Stir in the peas and cook for an additional 5 minutes.
8. Garnish with fresh parsley before serving.

Steel-Cut Oat Risotto with Mushrooms

Ingredients:

- 1 cup steel-cut oats
- 4 cups vegetable broth, kept warm
- 1 onion, finely chopped
- 2 cloves garlic, minced
- 2 cups mushrooms, sliced
- 1/3 cup nutritional yeast
- 1 tsp thyme
- 1 tsp rosemary
- Salt and pepper to taste
- Fresh chives for garnish

Instructions:

1. In a large pot, sauté the onion and garlic over medium heat until softened (use water or vegetable broth to avoid oil).
2. Add the mushrooms and cook until they release their moisture and become tender.
3. Stir in the steel-cut oats and cook for 1-2 minutes to lightly toast them.
4. Add 1 cup of vegetable broth at a time, cooking and stirring frequently. Add another cup only when the oats have absorbed the liquid. This process is similar to making traditional risotto.
5. After about 30 minutes, the oats should be creamy and tender.
6. Stir in the nutritional yeast, thyme, rosemary, salt, and pepper.
7. Garnish with fresh chives before serving.

Optional: Replace the mushrooms with one of the following, or feel free to add them to the recipe: grilled or roasted eggplant, sliced zucchini, artichoke hearts, firm tofu (cubed), small cauliflower florets, or sun-dried tomatoes.

Oat and Lentil Stuffed Peppers

Ingredients:

- 1 cup rolled oats
- 1/2 cup red lentils
- 4 large bell peppers
- 1 onion, finely chopped
- 2 cloves garlic, minced
- 1 zucchini, diced
- 1 cup diced tomatoes
- 1 tsp cumin
- 1 tsp oregano
- Salt and pepper to taste
- Fresh cilantro for garnish

Instructions:

1. Preheat your oven to 375°F (190°C) and line a baking dish with parchment paper.
2. Cook the red lentils and set aside.
3. Cut the tops off the bell peppers and remove the seeds.
4. In a large pan, sauté the onion and garlic over medium heat until softened (use water or vegetable broth to avoid oil).
5. Add the zucchini and cook until tender.
6. Stir in the rolled oats, cooked lentils, diced tomatoes, cumin, oregano, salt, and pepper. Cook until the oats are tender and the mixture is well combined.
7. Stuff the bell peppers with the oat and lentil mixture and place them in the prepared baking dish.
8. Cover with foil and bake for 30-35 minutes, until the peppers are tender.
9. Garnish with fresh cilantro before serving.

Sloppy Joes with Oats

Ingredients:

- 1 cup steel-cut oats or oat groats
- 1 cup water
- 1 cup French green lentils, well rinsed
- 1 medium carrot, grated
- 1/2 cup diced celery
- 1/2 cup diced red onion
- 2 cloves garlic, minced
- 1 bell pepper, diced
- 1/2 cup tomato sauce
- 1 tbsp tomato paste
- 1 tsp smoked paprika
- 1 tsp cumin
- Miso (sea salt) and pepper to taste

Instructions:

1. In a pot, bring the water to a boil. Add the oat groats and reduce the heat to low. Cover and simmer for about 50 minutes (steel-cut oats about 30 minutes) or until the oats are tender.
2. In a separate pot, cook the French green lentils (Rinse the lentils. In a saucepan, cover lentils with water by 2 inches. Bring water to a boil, then simmer on low for 20-30 minutes. Drain.

3. In a large pan, sauté the carrot, celery, red onion, garlic, and bell pepper in a small amount of water until they are soft.
4. Add the cooked oat groats and lentils to the pan with the vegetables.
5. Stir in the tomato sauce, tomato paste, smoked paprika, cumin, salt, and pepper.
6. Cook over medium heat for about 10 minutes, stirring occasionally.
7. Serve hot on whole grain buns with your favorite vegan toppings.

This recipe includes grated carrot and diced celery for added crunch and nutrition. The French green lentils provide a firmer texture that holds up well in the sloppy joe mixture.
Option: use cooked garbanzo beans (chickpeas) in place of the lentils.

Why did the **oats attend the cooking class?**

They wanted to learn how to roll with the dough!

The Great Oat Loaf: Meatless Loaves

Rolled Oats Vegetable Loaf

Ingredients:

- 2 cups rolled oats
- 1 cup mashed beans (any variety)
- 1 cup grated beetroot
- 1/2 cup finely chopped mushrooms (replace or add: zucchini, carrots, spinach, eggplant, and bell peppers)
- 1/4 cup nutritional yeast
- 2 tbsp tomato paste
- 1 tbsp soy sauce or tamari
- 1 tsp dried thyme
- 1 tsp smoked paprika
- Salt and pepper to taste

Instructions:

1. Preheat oven to 350°F (175°C).
2. In a large bowl, mix all ingredients until well combined.
3. Press the mixture into a loaf pan lined with parchment paper.
4. Bake for 45-50 minutes until the top is firm and slightly crispy.
5. Let it cool for 10 minutes before slicing.

Lentil & Walnut Loaf

Ingredients:

- 2 cups cooked green lentils
- 1 cup rolled oats, ground into flour
- 1/2 cup walnuts, finely chopped
- 1/2 cup grated carrots
- 1/2 cup finely chopped celery
- 1/2 cup finely chopped onion
- 2 cloves garlic, minced
- 2 tbsp tomato paste
- 2 tbsp soy sauce or tamari
- 2 tbsp ground flaxseed mixed with 6 tbsp water (flax egg)
- 1 tsp smoked paprika
- 1 tsp dried thyme
- Salt and pepper to taste

Instructions:

1. Preheat your oven to 375°F (190°C).
2. In a large bowl, mash the lentils until mostly smooth.
3. Stir in the ground oats, walnuts, carrots, celery, onion, and garlic.
4. Add the tomato paste, soy sauce, flax egg, smoked paprika, thyme, salt, and pepper. Mix well.
5. Press the mixture into a lined loaf 9x5-inch (23x13 cm) pan.
6. Bake for 45 minutes, or until the top is firm and slightly crispy.
7. Let it cool for 10 minutes before slicing.

Chickpea & Oat Groats Loaf

Ingredients:

- 2 cups cooked chickpeas
- 1 cup cooked oat groats
- 1/2 cup rolled oats
- 1/2 cup diced red bell pepper
- 1/2 cup diced mushrooms
- 1/4 cup chopped fresh parsley
- 2 cloves garlic, minced
- 2 tbsp ground flaxseed mixed with 6 tbsp water (flax egg)
- 1 tbsp balsamic vinegar
- 1 tsp dried oregano
- Salt and pepper to taste

Instructions:

1. Preheat your oven to 375°F (190°C).
2. In a food processor, pulse the chickpeas and oat groats until combined but still chunky.
3. Transfer to a large bowl and add the rolled oats, bell pepper, mushrooms, parsley, and garlic.
4. Stir in the flax egg, balsamic vinegar, oregano, salt, and pepper.
5. Form the mixture into a loaf shape on a parchment-lined baking tray.
6. Bake for 50 minutes, or until the loaf is golden and holds together well.
7. Allow to cool slightly before serving.

The Whole Grain Gourmet: Oat-Infused Salad Spectacular

Dive into a world where salads are reimagined and oats take center stage, creating a delightful fusion of textures and flavors. In this section, we celebrate the unsung heroes of the salad world, where vibrant vegetables, tangy dressings, and wholesome oats come together in a culinary ballet. These recipes showcase the humble oat in a new light, proving that salads need not be defined by leafy greens to be refreshing and delicious.

These salads are designed to impress, with oats adding a satisfying bite and a depth of flavor that elevates them from mere sides to the stars of the dining table.

So, ready your taste buds for a parade of oat-enriched salads that are as nutritious as they are indulgent. Let's toss up tradition and savor the oat-infused goodness in every spoonful!

> Oats have been cultivated by humans since ancient times. They were initially considered weeds until humans began intentionally cultivating them for food.

Oat Groat and Chickpea Salad

Ingredients:

- 1 cup oat groats
- 1 can (1 1/2 cup) drained chickpeas
- 1 cucumber, diced
- 1 bell pepper, diced
- 1/2 red onion, finely chopped
- 1 cup cherry tomatoes, halved
- 1/4 cup fresh parsley, chopped
- 1/4 cup fresh lemon juice
- 1 tsp ground cumin
- Salt and pepper to taste

Instructions:

1. Soak the oat groats in water for at least 4 hours or overnight.
2. Drain the oat groats and cook in a large pot with 2 cups of water for about 30-40 minutes, until tender. Drain any excess water and let cool.
3. In a large bowl, combine the cooked oat groats, chickpeas, cucumber, bell pepper, red onion, cherry tomatoes, and parsley.
4. In a small bowl, whisk together the lemon juice, cumin, salt, and pepper.
5. Pour the dressing over the salad and toss to combine.
6. Chill in the refrigerator for at least 30 minutes before serving.

Refreshing Oat Berry Salad

Ingredients:

- 1 cup rolled oats
- 2 cups water
- 1 cup mixed berries (strawberries, blueberries, raspberries)
- 1 cup baby spinach
- 1/4 cup chopped walnuts
- 1/4 cup fresh orange juice
- 1 tbsp balsamic vinegar
- A pinch of sea salt (optional)

Instructions:

1. Cook rolled oats in water until they are soft and fluffy. Let them cool.
2. In a large bowl, combine the cooled oats, mixed berries, and baby spinach.
3. In a small bowl, whisk together the orange juice, balsamic vinegar, and a pinch of sea salt to make the dressing.
4. Drizzle the dressing over the salad and toss gently.
5. Top with chopped walnuts before serving.

Why don't oats ever get lost?

Because they always oat-ientate themselves!

Savory Steel-Cut Oat Salad

Ingredients:

- 1 cup steel-cut oats
- 3 cups vegetable broth
- 1 cucumber, diced
- 1 tomato, diced
- 1/2 red onion, finely chopped
- 1/4 cup lemon juice
- 1 tsp dried mint
- Salt and pepper to taste

Instructions:

1. Cook steel-cut oats in vegetable broth until liquid is absorbed. Let them cool.
2. In a large bowl, mix the cooled oats with cucumber, tomato, and red onion.
3. For the dressing, combine lemon juice, dried mint, salt, and pepper.
4. Toss the salad with the dressing and let it sit for 10 minutes to absorb the flavors before serving.

Oat Groat Mediterranean Salad

Ingredients:

- 1 cup oat groats
- 2 cups water
- 1 cup cherry tomatoes, halved
- 1 cup cucumber, diced
- 1/2 cup kalamata olives, pitted and halved
- 1/4 cup chopped parsley
- 1/4 cup lemon juice
- 1 tsp dried oregano
- Salt and pepper to taste

Instructions:

1. Cook oat groats in water until tender. Drain any excess water and let them cool.
2. In a salad bowl, combine the oat groats with cherry tomatoes, cucumber, and kalamata olives.
3. Add chopped parsley, lemon juice, dried oregano, salt, and pepper.
4. Toss everything together and adjust seasoning if necessary.

Asian Oat and Edamame Salad

Ingredients:

- 1 cup cooked oat groats (chilled)
- 1 cup shelled edamame (cooked and cooled)
- 1 red bell pepper, diced
- 1 carrot, julienned
- 1/4 cup chopped green onions
- 2 tablespoons rice vinegar
- 1 tablespoon soy sauce (or tamari)
- 1 teaspoon grated ginger
- 1 clove garlic, minced
- Sesame seeds for garnish

Instructions:

1. In a large bowl, mix the oat groats, edamame, red bell pepper, carrot, and green onions.
2. In a small bowl, whisk together the rice vinegar, soy sauce, grated ginger, and minced garlic.
3. Pour the dressing over the salad and toss to coat evenly.
4. Sprinkle sesame seeds on top as a garnish.
5. Chill in the refrigerator for about an hour before serving to let the flavors develop.

Crisp Apple and Spinach Salad

Ingredients:

- 2 cups fresh spinach leaves
- 1 apple, cored and thinly sliced
- 1/4 cup chopped walnuts
- 1/4 cup dried cranberries
- 1/2 cup cooked and cooled steel-cut oats or oat groats
- 2 tablespoons balsamic vinegar
- 1 tablespoon fresh lemon juice
- **Optional:** A pinch of cinnamon for added flavor

Instructions:

1. In a large salad bowl, combine the spinach leaves and apple slices, cooked oats, chopped walnuts and dried cranberries.
2. In a small bowl, whisk together the balsamic vinegar and lemon juice. If desired, add a pinch of cinnamon.
3. Drizzle the dressing over the salad and toss gently to coat.
4. Serve immediately for the freshest taste.

Adding oats will give your salad a delightful chewy texture and extra nutrition. Enjoy!

Tangy Citrus Kale Salad

Ingredients:

- 2 cups chopped kale leaves; stems removed
- 1 orange, peeled and sectioned
- 1/4 cup sliced almonds
- 1/4 cup shredded carrot
- 1/2 cup cooked and cooled steel-cut oats or oat groats
- 2 tablespoons apple cider vinegar
- 1 tablespoon orange juice
- **Optional:** Freshly ground black pepper to taste

Instructions:

1. In a large salad bowl, combine the chopped kale, orange sections, sliced almonds, shredded carrot, and cooked oats.
2. In a small bowl, whisk together the apple cider vinegar and orange juice. Add freshly ground black pepper if desired.
3. Drizzle the dressing over the salad and toss gently to coat.
4. Serve immediately for the freshest taste.

These salads are light, refreshing, and packed with natural flavors, making them perfect for a healthy meal or side dish. Enjoy your nutritious greens!

Oat Inspirations: Sweet & Savory Bakes for the Family

Step into the world of savory satisfaction with our collection of baked oatmeal recipes that are not just side dishes, but star players for your main meals! Each dish is a canvas awaiting your personal touch—mix in a medley of your cherished fruits, vegetables and herbs to create a heartwarming, wholesome meal that the entire family will relish. These recipes are more than just nourishing; they're a celebration of flavor that brings everyone together around the dining table.

So, let's turn the page and embark on a culinary journey where oats take center stage, proving that they have a delicious place at any meal, any time of day. Bon appétit!

Blueberry Banana Baked Oatmeal

Ingredients:

- 2 cups rolled oats
- 1 1/2 cups unsweetened oat milk (or substitute)
- 2 ripe bananas, mashed
- 1 cup fresh or frozen blueberries
- 1 tsp vanilla extract
- 1 tsp ground cinnamon
- 1/2 tsp baking powder
- 1/4 tsp sea salt
- 1 tbsp chia seeds (optional)

Instructions:

1. Preheat your oven to 350°F (175°C) and lightly grease an 8x8 inches (20x20 cm) or 2-quart (1.9 liter) baking dish with non-stick cooking spray or line it with parchment paper.
2. In a large bowl, combine all of the ingredients. Mix well.
3. Pour the mixture into the prepared baking dish and spread it out evenly.
4. Bake for 35-40 minutes, until the top is golden brown and the oatmeal is set.
5. Allow to cool for a few minutes before serving. Serve warm or cold.

Classic Apple Cinnamon Baked Oatmeal

Ingredients:

- 2 cups rolled oats
- 1 1/2 cups unsweetened oat milk (or substitute)
- 1 cup unsweetened applesauce
- 1 apple, peeled and chopped
- 1/4 cup raisins
- 1/4 cup chopped walnuts (optional)
- 1 tsp ground cinnamon
- 1 tsp vanilla extract
- 1/2 tsp baking powder
- 1/4 tsp sea salt

Instructions:

1. Preheat your oven to 350°F (175°C) and lightly grease an 8x8 inches (20x20 cm) or 2-quart (1.9 liter) baking dish with non-stick cooking spray or line it with parchment paper.
2. In a large bowl, combine all of the ingredients. Mix well.
3. Pour the mixture into the prepared baking dish and spread it out evenly.
4. Bake for 35-40 minutes, until the top is golden brown and the oatmeal is set.
5. Allow to cool for a few minutes before serving. Serve warm or cold.

Peanut Butter and Banana Baked Oatmeal

Ingredients:

- 2 cups rolled oats
- 1 1/2 cups unsweetened oat milk (or substitute)
- 2 ripe bananas, mashed
- 1/4 cup peanut butter (or any nut butter)
- 1 tsp vanilla extract
- 1/2 tsp ground cinnamon
- 1/2 tsp baking powder
- 1/4 tsp sea salt

Instructions:

1. Preheat your oven to 350°F (175°C) and lightly grease an 8x8 inches (20x20 cm) or 2-quart (1.9 liter) baking dish with non-stick cooking spray or line it with parchment paper.
2. In a large bowl, combine all the ingredients. Mix well.
3. Pour the mixture into the prepared baking dish and spread it out evenly.
4. Bake for 35-40 minutes, until the top is golden brown and the oatmeal is set.
5. Allow to cool for a few minutes before serving. Serve warm or cold.

Pumpkin Spice Baked Oatmeal

Ingredients:

- 2 cups rolled oats
- 1 1/2 cups unsweetened oat milk (or substitute)
- 1 cup canned pumpkin puree (not pumpkin pie filling)
- 1/4 cup chopped dates
- 1/4 cup chopped pecans (optional)
- 1 tsp vanilla extract
- 1 1/2 tsp ground cinnamon
- 1/2 tsp ground nutmeg
- 1/2 tsp ground ginger
- 1/4 tsp ground cloves
- 1/2 tsp baking powder
- 1/4 tsp sea salt

Instructions:

1. Preheat your oven to 350°F (175°C) and lightly grease an 8x8 inches (20x20 cm) or 2-quart (1.9 liter) baking dish with non-stick cooking spray or line it with parchment paper.
2. In a large bowl, combine the rolled oats, oat milk, pumpkin puree, chopped dates, pecans (if using), vanilla extract, cinnamon, nutmeg, ginger, cloves, baking powder, and salt. Mix well.
3. Pour the mixture into the prepared baking dish and spread it out evenly.
4. Bake for 35-40 minutes, until the top is golden brown and the oatmeal is set.
5. Allow to cool for a few minutes before serving. Serve warm or cold.

6. Pour the mixture into the prepared baking dish and spread it out evenly.
7. Bake for 35-40 minutes, until the top is golden brown and the oatmeal is set.
8. Allow to cool for a few minutes before serving. Serve warm or cold.

> **Colonial America:** Oats were introduced to North America by European colonists in the 17th century. They became an important crop in the northern regions of the continent, where the climate was well-suited to their cultivation.

Mixed Berry Baked Oatmeal

Ingredients:

- 2 cups rolled oats
- 1 1/2 cups unsweetened oat milk (or substitute)
- 1/2 cup unsweetened applesauce
- 1 cup mixed berries (fresh or frozen)
- 1 tsp vanilla extract
- 1/2 tsp ground cinnamon
- 1/2 tsp baking powder
- 1/4 tsp sea salt

Instructions:

1. Preheat your oven to 350°F (175°C) and lightly grease an 8x8 inches (20x20 cm) or 2-quart (1.9 liter) baking dish with non-stick cooking spray or line it with parchment paper.
2. In a large bowl, combine the rolled oats, oat milk, applesauce, mixed berries, vanilla extract, cinnamon, baking powder, and salt. Mix well.
3. Pour the mixture into the prepared baking dish and spread it out evenly.
4. Bake for 35-40 minutes, until the top is golden brown and the oatmeal is set.
5. Allow to cool for a few minutes before serving. Serve warm or cold.
6. These baked oatmeal recipes are versatile and can be customized with your favorite fruits, nuts, and spices. They are perfect for a healthy breakfast or snack and can be prepared in advance for meal prep.

Savory Mushroom and Spinach Baked Oatmeal

Ingredients:

- 2 cups rolled oats
- 1 1/2 cups low sodium vegetable broth
- 1 cup unsweetened oat milk (or substitute)
- 1 cup chopped fresh spinach
- 1 cup chopped mushrooms
- 1 small onion, finely chopped
- 2 cloves garlic, minced
- 1 tbsp nutritional yeast
- 1 tsp dried thyme
- 1 tsp dried oregano
- 1/2 tsp ground black pepper
- 1/4 tsp sea salt

Instructions:

1. Preheat your oven to 375°F (190°C) and lightly grease an 8x8 inches (20x20 cm) or 2-quart (1.9 liter) baking dish with non-stick cooking spray or line it with parchment paper.
2. In a large skillet, sauté the chopped onion and garlic until fragrant and translucent.
3. Add the mushrooms and spinach to the skillet, cooking until the mushrooms are tender and the spinach is wilted. Remove from heat.
4. In a large bowl, combine the rolled oats, vegetable broth, oat milk, cooked vegetables, nutritional yeast, thyme, oregano, black pepper, and salt. Mix well.
5. Pour the mixture into the prepared baking dish and spread it out evenly.
6. Bake for 35-40 minutes, until the top is golden brown and the oatmeal is set.
7. Allow to cool for a few minutes before serving. Serve warm.

Tomato and Basil Baked Oatmeal

Ingredients:

- 2 cups rolled oats
- 1 1/2 cups low sodium vegetable broth
- 1 cup unsweetened oat milk (or substitute)
- 1 cup diced tomatoes (fresh or canned, no salt added)
- 1/2 cup fresh basil, chopped
- 1 small onion, finely chopped
- 2 cloves garlic, minced
- 1 tbsp nutritional yeast
- 1 tsp dried oregano
- 1 tsp dried basil
- 1/2 tsp ground black pepper
- 1/4 tsp sea salt

Instructions:

1. Preheat your oven to 375°F (190°C) and lightly grease an 8x8 inches (20x20 cm) or 2-quart (1.9 liter) baking dish with non-stick cooking spray or line it with parchment paper.
2. In a large skillet, sauté the chopped onion and garlic until fragrant and translucent.
3. In a large bowl, combine the rolled oats, vegetable broth, oat milk, diced tomatoes, fresh basil, cooked onion and garlic, nutritional yeast, dried oregano, dried basil, black pepper, and salt. Mix well.
4. Pour the mixture into the prepared baking dish and spread it out evenly.
5. Bake for 35-40 minutes, until the top is golden brown and the oatmeal is set.
6. Allow to cool for a few minutes before serving. Serve warm.

Cold Weather Crop: Oats are well-suited to colder climates and can tolerate lower temperatures than other cereal grains like wheat and barley. This makes them a popular crop in regions with short growing seasons or cool climates.

Savory Herb and Vegetable Baked Oatmeal

Ingredients:

- 2 cups rolled oats
- 1 1/2 cups low sodium vegetable broth
- 1 cup unsweetened oat milk (or substitute)
- 1 cup chopped mixed vegetables (such as bell peppers, zucchini, and carrots)
- 1 small onion, finely chopped
- 2 cloves garlic, minced
- 1 tbsp nutritional yeast
- 1 tsp dried rosemary
- 1/2 tsp ground black pepper
- 1/4 tsp sea salt

Instructions:

1. Preheat your oven to 375°F (190°C) and lightly grease an 8x8 inches (20x20 cm) or 2-quart (1.9 liter) baking dish with non-stick cooking spray or line it with parchment paper.
2. In a large skillet, sauté the chopped onion and garlic until fragrant and translucent.
3. Add the mixed vegetables to the skillet and cook until they are tender. Remove from heat.
4. In a large bowl, combine the rolled oats, vegetable broth, oat milk, cooked vegetables, nutritional yeast, thyme, rosemary, black pepper, and salt. Mix well.
5. Pour the mixture into the prepared baking dish and spread it out evenly.
6. Bake for 35-40 minutes, until the top is golden brown and the oatmeal is set.
7. Allow to cool for a few minutes before serving. Serve warm.

Savory Curry Baked Oatmeal

Ingredients:

- 2 cups rolled oats
- 1 1/2 cups low sodium vegetable broth
- 1 cup unsweetened coconut milk (or substitute)
- 1 cup diced tomatoes (fresh or canned, no salt added)
- 1 cup chopped spinach
- 1 small onion, finely chopped
- 2 cloves garlic, minced
- 1 tbsp curry powder
- 1 tsp ground cumin
- 1 tsp ground coriander
- 1/2 tsp ground turmeric
- 1/2 tsp ground black pepper
- 1/4 tsp sea salt

Instructions:

1. Preheat your oven to 375°F (190°C) and lightly grease an 8x8 inches (20x20 cm) or 2-quart (1.9 liter) baking dish with non-stick cooking spray or line it with parchment paper.
2. In a large skillet, sauté the chopped onion and garlic until fragrant and translucent.
3. Add the diced tomatoes and spinach to the skillet, cooking until the spinach is wilted. Remove from heat.
4. In a large bowl, combine the rolled oats, vegetable broth, coconut milk, cooked vegetables, curry powder, cumin, coriander, turmeric, black pepper, and salt. Mix well.
5. Pour the mixture into the prepared baking dish and spread it out evenly.
6. Bake for 35-40 minutes, until the top is golden brown and the oatmeal is set.
7. Allow to cool for a few minutes before serving. Serve warm.
8. These savory baked oatmeal recipes provide a delicious and nutritious alternative to traditional sweet oatmeal, making them perfect for main meals. Customize them with your favorite vegetables and herbs for a satisfying and healthy dish.

Pizza Baked Oatmeal

Ingredients:

- 2 cups rolled oats
- 1 1/2 cups low sodium vegetable broth
- 1 cup unsweetened oat milk (or substitute)
- 1 cup marinara sauce
- 1/2 cup chopped bell peppers
- 1/2 cup chopped onions
- 1/2 cup chopped mushrooms
- 1/4 cup sliced black olives
- 1/4 cup chopped tomatoes
- 1/4 cup nutritional yeast
- 2 tbsp chopped fresh basil
- 1 tsp dried oregano
- 1/2 tsp garlic powder
- 1/2 tsp onion powder
- 1/2 tsp crushed red pepper flakes (optional)
- 1/4 tsp sea salt

Instructions:

1. Preheat your oven to 375°F (190°C) and lightly grease an 8x8 inches (20x20 cm) or 2-quart (1.9 liter) baking dish with non-stick cooking spray or line it with parchment paper.
2. In a large bowl, combine the rolled oats, vegetable broth, oat milk, marinara sauce, bell peppers, onions, mushrooms, black olives, tomatoes, nutritional yeast, basil, oregano, garlic powder, onion powder, crushed red pepper flakes (if using), and salt. Mix well.
3. Pour the mixture into the prepared baking dish and spread it out evenly.
4. Bake for 35-40 minutes, until the top is golden brown and the oatmeal is set.
5. Allow to cool for a few minutes before serving. Serve warm, garnished with additional fresh basil if desired.

Optional – add some meat alternative from recipes in this book. (such as hamburger, pepperoni or sausage)

Taco Baked Oatmeal

Ingredients:

- 2 cups rolled oats
- 1 1/2 cups low sodium vegetable broth
- 1 cup unsweetened oat milk (or substitute)
- 1 cup black beans, drained and rinsed
- 1/2 cup corn kernels (fresh or frozen)
- 1/2 cup diced tomatoes
- 1/2 cup chopped bell peppers
- 1 small onion, finely chopped
- 2 cloves garlic, minced
- 1 tbsp chili powder
- 1 tsp ground cumin
- 1 tsp smoked paprika
- 1/2 tsp dried oregano
- 1/2 tsp ground black pepper
- 1/4 tsp miso or sea salt
- 1/4 cup chopped fresh cilantro

Instructions:

1. Preheat your oven to 375°F (190°C) and lightly grease an 8x8 inches (20x20 cm) or 2-quart (1.9 liter) baking dish with non-stick cooking spray or line it with parchment paper.
2. In a large skillet, sauté the chopped onion and garlic until fragrant and translucent.
3. In a large bowl, combine the rolled oats, vegetable broth, oat milk, black beans, corn, diced tomatoes, bell peppers, cooked onion and garlic, chili powder, cumin, smoked paprika, oregano, black pepper, and salt. Mix well.
4. Pour the mixture into the prepared baking dish and spread it out evenly.
5. Bake for 35-40 minutes, until the top is golden brown and the oatmeal is set.
6. Allow to cool for a few minutes before serving. Serve warm, garnished with fresh cilantro.

Environmental Benefits: Oats are considered an environmentally friendly crop because they require less fertilizer and pesticide use compared to other cereal grains. They also have deep root systems that help prevent soil erosion.

Mediterranean Baked Oatmeal

Ingredients:

- 2 cups rolled oats
- 1 1/2 cups low sodium vegetable broth
- 1 cup unsweetened oat milk (or substitute)
- 1 cup chopped spinach
- 1/2 cup chopped artichoke hearts (canned, drained, and rinsed)
- 1/2 cup chopped sun-dried tomatoes (not in oil)
- 1/4 cup sliced kalamata olives
- 1 small onion, finely chopped
- 2 cloves garlic, minced
- 1 tbsp nutritional yeast
- 1 tsp dried oregano
- 1 tsp dried basil
- 1/2 tsp ground black pepper
- 1/4 tsp sea salt

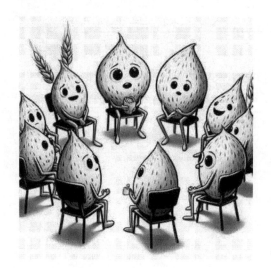

Instructions:

- Preheat your oven to 375°F (190°C) and lightly grease an 8x8 inches (20x20 cm) or 2-quart (1.9 liter) baking dish with non-stick cooking spray or line it with parchment paper.

1. In a large skillet, sauté the chopped onion and garlic until fragrant and translucent.
2. In a large bowl, combine the rolled oats, vegetable broth, oat milk, spinach, artichoke hearts, sun-dried tomatoes, olives, cooked onion and garlic, nutritional yeast, oregano, basil, black pepper, and salt. Mix well.
3. Pour the mixture into the prepared baking dish and spread it out evenly.
4. Bake for 35-40 minutes, until the top is golden brown and the oatmeal is set.
5. Allow to cool for a few minutes before serving. Serve warm.

Why did the oats join a support group?

Because they needed to vent their oat-rage!

Vegetable Pot Pie Baked Oatmeal

Ingredients:

- 2 cups rolled oats
- 1 1/2 cups low sodium vegetable broth
- 1 cup unsweetened oat milk (or substitute)
- 1 cup mixed vegetables (peas, carrots, green beans) frozen or fresh
- 1/2 cup chopped potatoes
- 1 small onion, finely chopped
- 2 cloves garlic, minced
- 1 tbsp nutritional yeast
- 1 tsp dried thyme
- 1 tsp dried rosemary
- 1/2 tsp ground black pepper
- 1/4 tsp Miso (or sea salt)

Instructions:

1. Preheat your oven to 375°F (190°C)
2. lightly grease an 8x8 inches (20x20 cm) or 2-quart (1.9 liter) baking dish with non-stick cooking spray or line it with parchment paper.
3. In a large skillet, sauté the chopped onion and garlic until fragrant and translucent.
4. Add the mixed vegetables and potatoes to the skillet, cooking until the vegetables are tender. Remove from heat.
5. In a large bowl, combine the rolled oats, vegetable broth, oat milk, cooked vegetables, nutritional yeast, thyme, rosemary, black pepper, and salt. Mix well.
6. Pour the mixture into the prepared baking dish and spread it out evenly.
7. Bake for 35-40 minutes, until the top is golden brown and the oatmeal is set.
8. Allow to cool for a few minutes before serving. Serve warm.

Italian Herb and Tomato Baked Oatmeal

Ingredients:

- 2 cups rolled oats
- 1 1/2 cups low sodium vegetable broth
- 1 cup unsweetened oat milk (or substitute)
- 1 cup diced tomatoes (fresh or canned, no salt added)
- 1/2 cup chopped zucchini
- 1/2 cup chopped bell peppers
- 1 small onion, finely chopped
- 2 cloves garlic, minced
- 1 tbsp nutritional yeast
- 1 tsp dried basil
- 1 tsp dried oregano
- 1/2 tsp dried thyme
- 1/2 tsp ground black pepper
- 1/4 tsp Miso (or sea salt) (optional)

Instructions:

1. Preheat your oven to 375°F (190°C) and lightly grease an 8x8 inches (20x20 cm) or 2-quart (1.9 liter) baking dish with non-stick cooking spray or line it with parchment paper.

2. In a large skillet, sauté the chopped onion and garlic until fragrant and translucent.

3. In a large bowl, combine the rolled oats, vegetable broth, oat milk, diced tomatoes, zucchini, bell peppers, cooked onion and garlic, nutritional yeast, basil, oregano, thyme, black pepper, and salt. Mix well.

4. Pour the mixture into the prepared baking dish and spread it out evenly.

5. Bake for 35-40 minutes, until the top is golden brown and the oatmeal is set.

6. Allow to cool for a few minutes before serving. Serve warm.

Personalize your oat-based baked delights by adding a mix of your preferred fruits, vegetables, and herbs to create a dish that's both tasty and healthful.

Oats afloat: Savory Soup Adventures

Grab your pot and let's simmer our way to soup with oats as a secret ingredient!

Hearty Oat Groat Stew

Ingredients:

- 1 cup oat groats
- 4 cups vegetable broth
- 1 cup diced tomatoes
- 1 cup diced carrots
- 1 cup chopped kale
- 3/4 cup diced celery
- 3/4 cup diced onion
- 3 cloves garlic, minced
- 1 tsp dried basil
- 1 tsp dried oregano
- Salt and pepper to taste

Instructions:

1. In a large pot, sauté onions, garlic, carrots, and celery with a splash of vegetable broth until softened.
2. Add the oat groats, diced tomatoes, basil, oregano, salt, and pepper.
3. Pour in the vegetable broth and bring to a boil.
4. Reduce heat, cover, and simmer for 40 minutes.
5. Add the chopped kale in the last 10 minutes of cooking.

Creamy Oat Groat Mushroom Soup

Ingredients:

- 1 cup oat groats
- 4 cups vegetable broth
- 2 cups sliced mushrooms
- 1 diced onion
- 2 cloves garlic, minced
- 1 cup unsweetened oat milk
- 1 tsp dried thyme
- Salt and pepper to taste

Instructions:

1. In a pot, sauté onion and garlic with a splash of vegetable broth until translucent.
2. Add mushrooms and cook until they release their moisture.
3. Stir in oat groats and vegetable broth, bring to a boil, then simmer for 30 minutes.
4. Blend half the soup with oat milk until creamy, then return to the pot.
5. Season with thyme, salt, and pepper, and simmer for another 10 minutes.

Hearty Steel-Cut Oats Chili

Ingredients:

- 1 cup steel-cut oats
- 4 cups vegetable broth
- 1 can diced tomatoes
- 1 can black beans, drained and rinsed
- 1 diced bell pepper
- 1 diced onion
- 2 cloves garlic, minced
- 1 tbsp chili powder
- 1 tsp cumin
- Salt and pepper to taste

Instructions:

1. In a large pot, sauté onion, garlic, and bell pepper with a splash of vegetable broth until softened.
2. Add chili powder and cumin, cook for another minute.
3. Stir in steel-cut oats, diced tomatoes, black beans, and vegetable broth.
4. Bring to a boil, then reduce heat and simmer for 25-30 minutes.
5. Season with salt and pepper, and serve with avocado or lime wedges.

Rolled Oats and Lentil Soup

Ingredients:

- 1 cup rolled oats
- 1 cup red lentils
- 6 cups vegetable broth
- 1 diced carrot
- 1 diced celery stalk
- 1 diced onion
- 2 cloves garlic, minced
- 1 tsp turmeric
- 1 tsp paprika
- Salt and pepper to taste

Instructions:

1. Rinse red lentils thoroughly.
2. In a pot, sauté onion, garlic, carrot, and celery with a splash of vegetable broth until soft.
3. Add turmeric and paprika, stir for a minute.
4. Add rolled oats, red lentils, and vegetable broth.
5. Bring to a boil, then simmer for 20 minutes or until lentils are soft.
6. Season with salt and pepper, and serve hot.

Savory Oat Gravy

Ingredients:

- 1/2 cup rolled oats
- 2 cups vegetable broth or water
- 1/4 cup finely chopped onion
- 2 cloves garlic, minced
- 1 tsp soy sauce or tamari (for depth of flavor)
- 1/2 tsp dried thyme
- 1/2 tsp dried sage
- Salt and pepper to taste

Instructions:

- **Prepare the Oats:**

1. Grind the rolled oats in a blender or food processor until they reach a fine, flour-like consistency.

Cook the Aromatics:

2. In a saucepan over medium heat, add a small amount of vegetable broth. Sauté the onion and garlic until translucent, adding more broth as needed to prevent sticking.

Make the Gravy:

3. Sprinkle the ground oat flour over the sautéed onions and garlic. Cook for a minute, stirring constantly.
4. Gradually pour in the remaining vegetable broth while continuously whisking to avoid lumps.
5. Add the soy sauce, thyme, and sage. Bring the mixture to a simmer.

Thicken the Gravy:

6. Reduce the heat and let the gravy simmer for about 5-7 minutes, or until it reaches your desired thickness. Stir occasionally.

Season and Serve:

7. Taste and adjust the seasoning with salt and pepper.

Serve hot over mashed potatoes, biscuits, or your favorite plant-based dishes.

Enjoy your healthy, homemade oat gravy!

Great Oat Boom: In the late 19th and early 20th centuries, oats experienced a significant surge in popularity due to their nutritional value and versatility. This period, known as the "great oat boom," saw increased oat production and consumption around the world.

What do you call an oat who's always happy?

A jolly roller!

Chapter 9: Oatmeal's Meaty Makeover: The Oat Incognito

Oat Burgers: The Grain That Reigns the Plain

Step into the realm of oat burgers, where the humble oat ascends the throne as the sovereign of the sandwich. This section is dedicated to the art of crafting the perfect oat-based patty, a regal replacement for the traditional hamburger that will delight the palates of peasants and kings alike.

Within these pages, you'll find recipes that transform oats into majestic patties, each with a unique blend of spices, herbs, and wholesome ingredients. Whether you're a loyal subject of the plant kingdom or a curious carnivore seeking a truce with vegetables, these oat patties promise satisfaction in every bite.

So, don your apron, and let's begin the coronation of oats in your kitchen. Long live the oat burger!

Savory Steel-Cut Oat Patties

Ingredients:

- 1 cup steel-cut oats
- 2 cups water
- 1/2 cup grated zucchini
- 1/2 cup grated carrot
- 1/4 cup finely chopped onion
- 2 tbsp ground flaxseed mixed with 6 tbsp water (flax egg)
- 1 tsp garlic powder
- 1 tsp onion powder
- 1 tsp paprika
- Salt and pepper to taste

Instructions:

1. Cook steel-cut oats in water until soft.
2. In a bowl, combine the cooked oats, grated zucchini, carrot, onion, flax egg, garlic powder, onion powder, paprika, salt, and pepper.
3. Form the mixture into patties.
4. Place patties on a parchment-lined baking sheet.
5. Bake in a preheated oven at 375°F (190°C) for 25 minutes, flipping halfway through, until golden and firm.
6. Serve with your favorite sauce or in a burger bun with toppings.

Rolled Oats Vegetable Burger

Ingredients:

- 1 cup rolled oats
- 1 can black beans, drained and rinsed
- 1 small onion, finely chopped
- 1 carrot, grated
- 1/2 cup chopped spinach
- 2 cloves garlic, minced
- 2 tbsp ground flaxseed mixed with 6 tbsp water (flax egg)
- 1 tsp cumin
- 1 tsp smoked paprika
- Salt and pepper to taste
- Whole wheat burger buns

Instructions:

1. Preheat your oven to 375°F (190°C) and line a baking sheet with parchment paper.
2. In a large bowl, mash the black beans with a fork or potato masher until mostly smooth.
3. Add the rolled oats, onion, carrot, spinach, garlic, flax egg, cumin, smoked paprika, salt, and pepper.
4. Mix until well combined. If the mixture is too wet, add more oats; if too dry, add a bit of water or vegetable broth.
5. Shape the mixture into patties and place them on the prepared baking sheet.
6. Bake for 25-30 minutes, flipping halfway through, until the burgers are firm and golden brown.
7. Serve on whole wheat buns with your favorite toppings.

Black Bean and Oat Burgers

Ingredients:

- 1 cup rolled oats
- 1 can black beans, drained and rinsed
- 1 small onion, finely chopped
- 2 cloves garlic, minced
- 1/2 cup corn kernels (fresh or frozen)
- 1/2 cup grated carrot
- 1 tbsp ground flaxseed mixed with 3 tbsp water (flax egg)
- 1 tsp cumin
- 1 tsp smoked paprika
- Salt and pepper to taste

Instructions:

1. Preheat your oven to 375°F (190°C) and line a baking sheet with parchment paper.

2. In a large bowl, mash the black beans with a fork or potato masher until mostly smooth.

3. Add the rolled oats, onion, garlic, corn, grated carrot, flax egg, cumin, smoked paprika, salt, and pepper.

4. Mix until well combined. If the mixture is too wet, add more oats; if too dry, add a bit of water or vegetable broth.

5. Shape the mixture into burger patties and place them on the prepared baking sheet.

6. Bake for 25-30 minutes, flipping halfway through, until the burgers are firm and golden brown.

7. Serve on whole wheat buns with your favorite toppings.

Sweet Potato and Steel-Cut Oat Burgers

Ingredients:

- 1 cup steel-cut oats
- 1 large sweet potato, cooked and mashed
- 1 small onion, finely chopped
- 2 cloves garlic, minced
- 1/2 cup cooked quinoa
- 1/4 cup chopped fresh cilantro
- 1 tsp cumin
- 1 tsp chili powder

- Salt and pepper to taste

Instructions:

1. Cook the steel-cut oats and let cool slightly.

2. Preheat your oven to 375°F (190°C) and line a baking sheet with parchment paper.

3. In a large bowl, combine the cooked oats, mashed sweet potato, onion, garlic, cooked quinoa, cilantro, cumin, chili powder, salt, and pepper.

4. Mix until well combined. If the mixture is too wet, add more oats; if too dry, add a bit of water or vegetable broth.

5. Shape the mixture into burger patties and place them on the prepared baking sheet.

6. Bake for 25-30 minutes, flipping halfway through, until the burgers are firm and golden brown.

7. Serve on whole wheat buns with your favorite toppings.

Chickpea and Oat Groat Burgers

Ingredients:

- 1 cup oat groats
- 1 can (1 1/2 cup) chickpeas, drained and rinsed
- 1 small zucchini, grated
- 1 small onion, finely chopped
- 2 cloves garlic, minced
- 1/4 cup chopped fresh parsley
- 1 tbsp ground flaxseed mixed with 3 tbsp water (flax egg)
- 1 tsp cumin
- 1 tsp coriander
- Salt and pepper to taste

Instructions:

1. Rinse the oat groats and soak them in water for at least 4 hours or overnight.
2. Drain the oat groats and cook in a large pot with 2 cups of water for about 30-40 minutes, until tender. Drain any excess water and let cool slightly.
3. Preheat your oven to 375°F (190°C) and line a baking sheet with parchment paper.
4. In a large bowl, mash the chickpeas with a fork or potato masher until mostly smooth.
5. Add the cooked oat groats, grated zucchini, onion, garlic, parsley, flax egg, cumin, coriander, salt, and pepper.
6. Mix until well combined. If the mixture is too wet, add more oats; if too dry, add a bit of water or vegetable broth.
7. Shape the mixture into burger patties and place them on the prepared baking sheet.
8. Bake for 25-30 minutes, flipping halfway through, until the burgers are firm and golden brown.

Lentil and Rolled Oat Burgers

Ingredients:

- 1 cup rolled oats
- 1 cup cooked green or brown lentils
- 1 small carrot, grated
- 1 small onion, finely chopped
- 2 cloves garlic, minced
- 1/2 cup chopped spinach
- 1 tbsp ground flaxseed mixed with 3 tbsp water (flax egg)
- 1 tsp thyme
- 1 tsp smoked paprika
- Salt and pepper to taste

Instructions:

1. Preheat your oven to 375°F (190°C) and line a baking sheet with parchment paper.
2. In a large bowl, mash the cooked lentils with a fork or potato masher until mostly smooth.
3. Add the rolled oats, grated carrot, onion, garlic, spinach, flax egg, thyme, smoked paprika, salt, and pepper.
4. Mix until well combined. If the mixture is too wet, add more oats; if too dry, add a bit of water or vegetable broth.
5. Shape the mixture into burger patties and place them on the prepared baking sheet.
6. Bake for 25-30 minutes, flipping halfway through, until the burgers are firm and golden brown.
7. Serve on whole wheat buns with your favorite toppings.

Oats Incognito: Masquerading as Meats

In this innovative section, we delve into the world of oats in disguise, where they mimic the flavors and textures of our favorite meaty morsels. Oats take on new identities, transforming into succulent sausages, punchy pepperoni, and tantalizing taco meat. These recipes are a covert operation in culinary creativity, proving that oats have the power to infiltrate traditional meat dishes with plant-based prowess. Each recipe is a masterclass in deception, blending oats with bold spices and clever techniques to create alternatives that could fool even the most discerning of carnivores. If you love the challenge of cooking with oats, these oat-based meats are a delicious ruse that will bring intrigue and delight to your table. So, let's embark on this undercover culinary adventure together, and discover just how versatile oats can be when they step into the world of sausages, pepperoni, and taco meat. Prepare to be amazed as oats go incognito!

Sausage Patties

Ingredients:

- 1 cup rolled oats
- 1 cup cooked black beans, drained and rinsed
- 1/2 cup cooked quinoa
- 1 small onion, finely chopped
- 2 cloves garlic, minced
- 2 tbsp ground flaxseed mixed with 6 tbsp water (flax egg)
- 1 tbsp soy sauce or tamari
- 1 tsp smoked paprika
- 1 tsp fennel seeds, crushed
- 1 tsp dried sage
- 1 tsp dried thyme
- 1/2 tsp ground rosemary
- 1/2 tsp black pepper
- 1/2 tsp sea salt
- 1 tsp garlic powder (optional)
- 1/4 tsp red pepper flakes (optional)
- 1/2 teaspoon Cumin (optional)
- 1/2 teaspoon Coriander (optional)
- 1/2 teaspoon Mustard Powder (optional)
- 1-2 tbsp maple syrup or 1 tsp maple extract (optional)

Instructions:

1. Preheat your oven to 375°F (190°C) and line a baking sheet with parchment paper.
2. In a large bowl, mash the black beans until mostly smooth.
3. Add the cooked quinoa, rolled oats, onion, garlic, flax egg, soy sauce or tamari, smoked paprika, fennel seeds, sage, thyme, black pepper, salt, and red pepper flakes (if using).
4. Mix until well combined. If the mixture is too wet, add more oats; if too dry, add a bit of water or vegetable broth.
5. Shape the mixture into patties and place them on the prepared baking sheet.
6. Bake for 20-25 minutes, flipping halfway through, until the patties are firm and golden brown.
7. Serve with your favorite breakfast sides or on a biscuit as a sausage sandwich.

Sausage Crumbles

Ingredients:

- 1 cup rolled oats
- 1 cup cooked lentils (brown or green)
- 1 small onion, finely chopped
- 2 cloves garlic, minced
- 2 tbsp ground flaxseed mixed with 6 tbsp water (flax egg)
- 1 tbsp soy sauce or tamari

- 1 tsp smoked paprika
- 1 tsp ground fennel seeds
- 1 tsp dried oregano
- 1 tsp dried basil
- 1/2 tsp black pepper
- 1/2 tsp sea salt
- 1/4 tsp cayenne pepper (optional)

Instructions:

1. Preheat your oven to 375°F (190°C) and line a baking sheet with parchment paper.
2. In a large bowl, mash the cooked lentils with a fork or potato masher until mostly smooth.
3. Add the rolled oats, onion, garlic, flax egg, soy sauce or tamari, smoked paprika, ground fennel seeds, oregano, basil, black pepper, salt, and cayenne pepper (if using).
4. Mix until well combined. If the mixture is too wet, add more oats; if too dry, add a bit of water or vegetable broth.
5. Spread the mixture evenly on the prepared baking sheet.
6. Bake for 25-30 minutes, stirring halfway through, until the crumbles are browned and slightly crispy.

7. Use the crumbles in tacos, pasta dishes, salads, or as a topping for pizzas.

Italian Sausage Patties

Ingredients:

- 1 cup oat groats, cooked and cooled
- 1 cup cooked chickpeas, drained and rinsed
- 1 small onion, finely chopped
- 2 cloves garlic, minced
- 1/2 cup chopped fresh parsley
- 2 tbsp ground flaxseed mixed with 6 tbsp water (flax egg)
- 1 tbsp soy sauce or tamari
- 1 tsp fennel seeds, crushed
- 1 tsp dried basil
- 1 tsp dried oregano
- 1/2 tsp crushed red pepper flakes
- 1/2 tsp black pepper
- 1/2 tsp sea salt

Instructions:

1. Preheat your oven to 375°F (190°C) and line a baking sheet with parchment paper.
2. In a large bowl, mash the chickpeas with a fork or potato masher until mostly smooth.

3. Add the cooked oat groats, onion, garlic, parsley, flax egg, soy sauce or tamari, fennel seeds, basil, oregano, crushed red pepper flakes, black pepper, and salt.
4. Mix until well combined. If the mixture is too wet, add more oat groats; if too dry, add a bit of water or vegetable broth.
5. Shape the mixture into patties and place them on the prepared baking sheet.
6. Bake for 20-25 minutes, flipping halfway through, until the patties are firm and golden brown.
7. Serve with marinara sauce, on a bun, or as a side to pasta.

Spicy Sausage Crumbles

Ingredients:

- 1 cup steel-cut oats, cooked and cooled
- 1 cup cooked brown rice
- 1 small bell pepper, finely chopped
- 1 small onion, finely chopped
- 2 cloves garlic, minced
- 2 tbsp ground flaxseed mixed with 6 tbsp water (flax egg)
- 1 tbsp soy sauce or tamari
- 1 tsp smoked paprika
- 1 tsp ground cumin
- 1 tsp chili powder
- 1/2 tsp black pepper
- 1/2 tsp sea salt
- 1/4 tsp cayenne pepper

Instructions:

1. Preheat your oven to 375°F (190°C) and line a baking sheet with parchment paper.
2. In a large bowl, combine the cooked steel-cut oats and brown rice.
3. Add the bell pepper, onion, garlic, flax egg, soy sauce or tamari, smoked paprika, ground cumin, chili powder, black pepper, salt, and cayenne pepper.
4. Mix until well combined. If the mixture is too wet, add more steel-cut oats; if too dry, add a bit of water or vegetable broth.
5. Spread the mixture evenly on the prepared baking sheet.
6. Bake for 25-30 minutes, stirring halfway through, until the crumbles are browned and slightly crispy.
7. Use the crumbles in burritos, salads, casseroles, or as a filling for stuffed vegetables.

Baked Pepperoni Slices

Ingredients:

- 1 cup rolled oats
- 1 cup cooked chickpeas, drained and rinsed
- 1 small onion, finely chopped
- 2 cloves garlic, minced
- 1/4 cup tomato paste
- 2 tbsp ground flaxseed mixed with 6 tbsp water (flax egg)
- 1 tbsp soy sauce or tamari
- 1 tbsp apple cider vinegar
- 2 tsp smoked paprika
- 2 tsp ground fennel seeds
- 1 tsp dried oregano
- 1 tsp dried thyme
- 1 tsp ground black pepper
- 1/2 tsp cayenne pepper
- 1/2 tsp sea salt

Instructions:

1. Preheat your oven to 375°F (190°C) and line a baking sheet with parchment paper.

> **World Oat Crop:** Today, oats are primarily grown in temperate regions around the world, including North America, Europe, and Australia.

2. In a food processor, combine the rolled oats, chickpeas, onion, garlic, tomato paste, flax egg, soy sauce or tamari, apple cider vinegar, smoked paprika, ground fennel seeds, oregano, thyme, black pepper, cayenne pepper, and salt.
3. Pulse until the mixture is well combined and forms a dough-like consistency. If the mixture is too dry, add a bit of water or vegetable broth; if too wet, add more oats.
4. Transfer the mixture to a sheet of parchment paper and roll it into a log about 1-2 inches in diameter.
5. Wrap the log in parchment paper and refrigerate for at least 1 hour to firm up.
6. Once firm, slice the log into thin pepperoni rounds.
7. Arrange the slices on the prepared baking sheet and bake for 15-20 minutes, flipping halfway through, until the edges are slightly crispy and the slices are browned.
8. Allow the slices to cool before using on pizzas, in sandwiches, or as a snack.

Pepperoni Crumbles

Ingredients:

- 1 cup steel-cut oats, cooked and cooled
- 1 cup cooked lentils (brown or green)
- 1 small bell pepper, finely chopped
- 1 small onion, finely chopped
- 2 cloves garlic, minced
- 2 tbsp ground flaxseed mixed with 6 tbsp water (flax egg)
- 2 tbsp tomato paste
- 1 tbsp soy sauce or tamari
- 1 tbsp apple cider vinegar
- 2 tsp smoked paprika
- 2 tsp ground fennel seeds
- 1 tsp dried oregano
- 1 tsp dried thyme
- 1 tsp ground black pepper
- 1/2 tsp cayenne pepper
- 1/2 tsp sea salt

Instructions:

1. Preheat your oven to 375°F (190°C) and line a baking sheet with parchment paper.
2. In a large bowl, combine the cooked steel-cut oats and lentils.
3. Add the bell pepper, onion, garlic, flax egg, tomato paste, soy sauce or tamari, apple cider vinegar, smoked paprika, ground fennel seeds, oregano, thyme, black pepper, cayenne pepper, and salt.
4. Mix until well combined. If the mixture is too wet, add more steel-cut oats; if too dry, add a bit of water or vegetable broth.
5. Spread the mixture evenly on the prepared baking sheet.
6. Bake for 25-30 minutes, stirring halfway through, until the crumbles are browned and slightly crispy.
7. Use the crumbles on pizzas, in pasta dishes, salads, or as a topping for casseroles.

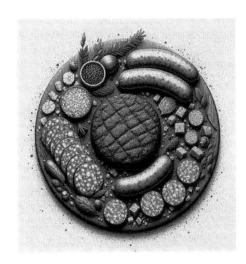

Sweet Potato and Oat Pepperoni Slices

Ingredients:

- 1 cup rolled oats
- 1 large sweet potato, cooked and mashed
- 1 small onion, finely chopped
- 2 cloves garlic, minced
- 1/4 cup tomato paste
- 2 tbsp ground flaxseed mixed with 6 tbsp water (flax egg)
- 1 tbsp soy sauce or tamari
- 1 tbsp apple cider vinegar
- 2 tsp smoked paprika
- 2 tsp ground fennel seeds
- 1 tsp dried basil
- 1 tsp dried thyme
- 1 tsp ground black pepper
- 1/2 tsp cayenne pepper
- 1/2 tsp sea salt

Instructions:

1. Preheat your oven to 375°F (190°C) and line a baking sheet with parchment paper.
2. In a food processor, combine the rolled oats, mashed sweet potato, onion, garlic, tomato paste, flax egg, soy sauce or tamari, apple cider vinegar, smoked paprika, ground fennel seeds, basil, thyme, black pepper, cayenne pepper, and salt.
3. Pulse until the mixture is well combined and forms a dough-like consistency. If the mixture is too dry, add a bit of water or vegetable broth; if too wet, add more oats.
4. Transfer the mixture to a sheet of parchment paper and roll it into a log about 1-2 inches in diameter.
5. Wrap the log in parchment paper and refrigerate for at least 1 hour to firm up.
6. Once firm, slice the log into thin pepperoni rounds.
7. Arrange the slices on the prepared baking sheet and bake for 15-20 minutes, flipping halfway through, until the edges are slightly crispy and the slices are browned.
8. Allow the slices to cool before using on pizzas, in sandwiches, or as a snack.

How do oats greet each other?

"Hey there, oat-migos!"

The Oatvolution: Ground Beef Reimagined

Embark on a culinary Oatvolution where the versatility of oats is unleashed as a stand-in for ground beef. These recipes are your gateway to reimagining classic dishes, offering a plant-based twist that's not only delicious but also environmentally friendly. From tacos to meatballs, our oat-based blends mimic the texture and heartiness of ground beef, ensuring that every bite is packed with flavor and goodness. Whether you're a committed or just looking to mix things up, these creations are here to revolutionize your meals and tantalize your taste buds!

Black Bean and Oat Ground Taco "Beef"

Ingredients:

- 1 cup rolled oats
- 1 cup cooked black beans, drained and rinsed
- 1 small bell pepper, finely chopped
- 1 small onion, finely chopped
- 2 cloves garlic, minced
- 1 tbsp soy sauce or tamari
- 1 tbsp tomato paste
- 1 tsp smoked paprika
- 1 1/2 tsp chili powder
- 1 tsp ground cumin
- 1/2 tsp black pepper
- 1/2 tsp sea salt

Instructions:

1. Preheat your oven to 375°F (190°C) and line a baking sheet with parchment paper.
2. In a large bowl, mash the black beans with a fork or potato masher until mostly smooth.
3. Add the rolled oats, bell pepper, onion, garlic, soy sauce or tamari, tomato paste, smoked paprika, chili powder, cumin, black pepper, and salt.
4. Mix until well combined. If the mixture is too wet, add more oats; if too dry, add a bit of water or vegetable broth.
5. Spread the mixture evenly on the prepared baking sheet.
6. Bake for 25-30 minutes, stirring halfway through, until the mixture is browned and slightly crispy.
7. Use as a ground beef substitute in burritos, shepherd's pie, stuffed peppers, or any dish that calls for ground beef.

Spicy Oat and Bean Taco Filling

Ingredients:

- 1 cup rolled oats
- 1 can black beans, drained and rinsed
- 1 cup vegetable broth
- 1 tbsp soy sauce or tamari
- 1 tbsp tomato paste
- 1 tsp chili powder
- 1 tsp cumin
- 1 tsp smoked paprika
- 1/2 tsp garlic powder
- 1/2 tsp onion powder
- Salt and pepper to taste

Instructions:

1. In a skillet over medium heat, add the rolled oats and toast them dry until they are golden brown.
2. Mash the black beans with a fork and add them to the skillet with the oats.
3. Stir in the vegetable broth, soy sauce, tomato paste, and all the spices.
4. Cook the mixture until the liquid is absorbed and the oats are soft, about 10 minutes.
5. Adjust seasoning with salt and pepper.

Lentil and Steel-Cut Oats Taco "Meat"

Ingredients:

- 1 cup steel-cut oats
- 1 cup red lentils
- 3 cups water
- 1 tbsp soy sauce or tamari
- 1 tbsp nutritional yeast
- 1 tsp chili powder
- 1 tsp cumin
- 1/2 tsp coriander
- 1/2 tsp smoked paprika
- Salt and pepper to taste

Instructions:

1. Rinse the red lentils and cook them in water until they start to break down, about 15 minutes.
2. Add the steel-cut oats and continue to cook, adding more water, if necessary, until both the lentils and oats are soft.
3. Stir in the soy sauce, nutritional yeast, and spices, cooking for another 5 minutes until the mixture thickens.
4. Season with salt and pepper to your liking.
5. Serve as a hearty taco filling with diced tomatoes, shredded lettuce, and salsa.

Savory Oat Groat "Meat"

Ingredients:

- 1 cup oat groats
- 2 cups vegetable broth
- 1 tbsp soy sauce or tamari
- 1 tsp garlic powder
- 1 tsp onion powder
- 1 tsp cumin
- 1/2 tsp chili flakes (optional for heat)
- Salt and pepper to taste

Instructions:

1. Cook the oat groats in the vegetable broth until they are tender and the broth is absorbed, about 30 minutes.
2. Once cooked, lightly mash the oat groats with a fork to create a textured "meat" consistency.
3. Stir in the soy sauce and all the spices, cooking for an additional 5 minutes to blend the flavors.
4. Taste and adjust the seasoning with salt and pepper.
5. Use this savory oat groat mixture as a filling for tacos, complemented by your choice of toppings.

Lentil and Oat Ground "Beef"

Ingredients:

- 1 cup rolled oats
- 1 cup cooked green or brown lentils
- 1 medium onion, finely chopped
- 2 cloves garlic, minced
- 1/2 cup finely chopped mushrooms
- 2 tbsp soy sauce or tamari
- 1 tbsp tomato paste
- 1 tsp smoked paprika
- 1 tsp dried thyme
- 1 tsp ground cumin
- 1/2 tsp black pepper
- 1/2 tsp sea salt
- 1/4 tsp red pepper flakes (optional)

Instructions:

1. Preheat your oven to 375°F (190°C) and line a baking sheet with parchment paper.
2. In a large bowl, combine the rolled oats, cooked lentils, onion, garlic, mushrooms, soy sauce or tamari, tomato paste, smoked paprika, thyme, cumin, black pepper, salt, and red pepper flakes (if using).

3. Mix until well combined. If the mixture is too wet, add more oats; if too dry, add a bit of water or vegetable broth.

4. Spread the mixture evenly on the prepared baking sheet.

5. Bake for 25-30 minutes, stirring halfway through, until the mixture is browned and slightly crispy.

6. Use as a ground beef substitute in tacos, spaghetti sauce, lasagna, or any dish that calls for ground beef.

Chickpea and Oat Groat Ground "Beef"

Ingredients:

- 1 cup oat groats, cooked and cooled
- 1 cup cooked chickpeas, drained and rinsed
- 1 small carrot, grated
- 1 medium onion, finely chopped
- 2 cloves garlic, minced
- 1 tbsp soy sauce or tamari
- 1 tbsp tomato paste
- 1 tsp smoked paprika
- 1 tsp dried oregano
- 1 tsp ground cumin
- 1/2 tsp black pepper
- 1/2 tsp sea salt

Instructions:

1. Cook the oat groats and let cool slightly.

2. Preheat your oven to 375°F (190°C) and line a baking sheet with parchment paper.

3. In a large bowl, mash the chickpeas with a fork or potato masher until mostly smooth.

4. Add the cooked oat groats, grated carrot, onion, garlic, soy sauce or tamari, tomato paste, smoked paprika, oregano, cumin, black pepper, and salt.

5. Mix until well combined. If the mixture is too wet, add more oat groats; if too dry, add a bit of water or vegetable broth.

6. Spread the mixture evenly on the prepared baking sheet.

7. Bake for 25-30 minutes, stirring halfway through, until the mixture is browned and slightly crispy.

8. Use as a ground beef substitute in casseroles, meatballs, vegetable burgers, or any dish that calls for ground beef.

Mushroom and Steel-Cut Oat Ground "Beef"

Ingredients:

- 1 cup steel-cut oats, cooked and cooled
- 2 cups finely chopped mushrooms
- 1 medium onion, finely chopped
- 2 cloves garlic, minced
- 1 tbsp soy sauce or tamari
- 1 tbsp tomato paste
- 1 tsp smoked paprika
- 1 tsp dried thyme
- 1 tsp ground black pepper
- 1/2 tsp sea salt

Instructions:

1. Cook the steel-cut oats and let cool slightly.
2. Preheat your oven to 375°F (190°C) and line a baking sheet with parchment paper.
3. In a large bowl, combine the cooked steel-cut oats, mushrooms, onion, garlic, soy sauce or tamari, tomato paste, smoked paprika, thyme, black pepper, and salt.
4. Mix until well combined. If the mixture is too wet, add more steel-cut oats; if too dry, add a bit of water or vegetable broth.
5. Spread the mixture evenly on the prepared baking sheet.
6. Bake for 25-30 minutes, stirring halfway through, until the mixture is browned and slightly crispy.
7. Use as a ground beef substitute in stir-fries, tacos, chili, or any dish that calls for ground beef.

Note:

For the upcoming recipes featuring our oat-based ground 'beef,' you're encouraged to use the suggested recipe or choose from any of the alternatives highlighted earlier to tailor the dish to your personal taste.

Lentil and Oat Meatballs

Ingredients:

- 1 batch Lentil and Oat Ground "Beef"
- 1 tbsp tomato paste
- 1 tbsp flaxseed meal
- 1/4 cup rolled oats
- 2 tbsp nutritional yeast
- 1 tbsp soy sauce or tamari
- 1 tsp dried basil
- 1 tsp dried oregano
- 1 tsp garlic powder
- Salt and pepper to taste
- 1 tbsp Worcestershire sauce (optional)
- Marinara sauce, for serving

Instructions:

1. Preheat your oven to 375°F (190°C) and line a baking sheet with parchment paper.
2. In a large bowl, combine the Lentil and Oat Ground "Beef" with flaxseed meal, tomato paste, rolled oats, nutritional yeast, soy sauce or tamari, basil, oregano, garlic powder, salt, and pepper.
3. Mix until well combined, then shape the mixture into golf ball-sized meatballs and place them on the prepared baking sheet.
4. Bake for 25-30 minutes, until the meatballs are browned and cooked through.
5. Serve the meatballs with marinara sauce over pasta or as a sub sandwich filling.

How do oats keep in touch?

Through the oaternet!

Black Bean and Oat Tacos

Ingredients:

- 1 batch Black Bean and Oat Ground "Beef"
- 8 small tortillas (corn or flour)
- 1 avocado, sliced
- 1 cup shredded lettuce
- 1 tomato, diced
- 1/4 cup chopped fresh cilantro
- Lime wedges, for serving
- Hot sauce, for serving

Instructions:

1. Heat the Black Bean and Oat Ground "Beef" in a skillet over medium heat until heated through.
2. Warm the tortillas in a dry skillet or microwave.
3. Assemble the tacos by placing a spoonful of the ground "beef" mixture onto each tortilla.
4. Top with avocado slices, shredded lettuce, diced tomato, and chopped cilantro.
5. Squeeze lime juice over the top and serve with hot sauce on the side.

Chapter 10: The Versatile Oat: Baking with Oat Flour

Welcome to the enchanting world of oat flour, where every sprinkle is a step into a realm of endless possibilities! This chapter is a treasure trove of recipes that will take you on a culinary journey far beyond the familiar shores of breads and pancakes. Unleash the magic within these pages and discover how oat flour can elevate the humble cracker to a crispy delight, transform tortillas into a wrap star, turn pizza crusts into a canvas for your wildest toppings, and morph muffins into morsels of joy. So, dust off your apron, preheat your oven, and let's bake our way to oat flour glory!

Making Oat Flour

From Oat Groats:

1. **Grain Grinder:** If you have a grain grinder, this is the best option for turning oat groats into flour. Simply feed the groats into the grinder and process them until you achieve a fine powder.

2. **High-Powered Blender:** A high-powered blender can also handle oat groats. Blend on high speed until the groats become a fine powder. You may need to stop and stir occasionally to ensure even grinding.

3. **Food Processor:** While not as efficient as a grain grinder or blender, a food processor can still do the job. Process the groats until they reach a powdery consistency, scraping down the sides as needed.

From Steel-Cut Oats:

1. **Coffee Grinder:** A coffee grinder is perfect for smaller batches of steel-cut oats. Grind the oats until they are fine, working in batches if necessary.

2. **Blender/Food Processor:** As with oat groats, use a blender or food processor to grind steel-cut oats into flour, ensuring you give the machine breaks to prevent overheating.

From Rolled Oats:

1. **Blender/Food Processor:** Rolled oats are softer and easier to grind. Use a blender or food processor to

2. turn them into flour in less time than groats or steel-cut oats.

3. **Coffee Grinder:** For small quantities, a coffee grinder can quickly turn rolled oats into flour.

Storage Suggestions:

- Store the oat flour in an airtight container to keep it fresh.

- Keep it in a cool, dry place away from direct sunlight, like a pantry or cupboard.

- For longer-term storage, you can refrigerate or freeze the oat flour. Just make sure it's in a sealed container to prevent moisture from getting in.

- Label the container with the date of grinding so you can keep track of freshness.

Additional Tips:

- Sift the flour after grinding to ensure a fine texture, especially if using it for delicate baked goods.

- If you find the flour is not as fine as you'd like, you can re-grind the coarser bits.

- Remember that homemade oat flour may have a shorter shelf life than store-bought flour due to the lack of preservatives, so it's best used within a few months.

With these methods, you can easily create oat flour at home using the tools you have available, and store it properly for future use in your recipes.

Tips for Baking Bread with Oat Flour:

- **Moisture:** Oat flour tends to absorb more moisture than other flours. Ensure your dough is hydrated enough to prevent dryness.

- **Kneading:** Knead the dough well to develop the gluten from the whole wheat flour, which helps give structure to the bread.

- **Rising:** Allow the dough to rise fully during both proofing stages to ensure a good texture and rise in the final loaf.

Oats in Sports Nutrition: Oats are a favorite among athletes and fitness enthusiasts due to their slow-releasing energy and high carbohydrate content. They are often consumed as part of pre-workout meals or snacks to provide sustained energy during exercise.

The Yeast of Our Worries: A Journey Through Artisanal Bread Making

Basic Oat Flour Bread

Ingredients:

- 3 cups oat flour
- 1 cup whole wheat flour
- 2 1/4 teaspoons (1 packet) active dry yeast
- 1 1/2 teaspoons salt
- 2 tablespoons honey
- 1 1/2 cups warm water (110°F/45°C)

Instructions:

1. In a large mixing bowl, combine flours, and salt.
2. In a small bowl, dissolve the honey in warm water. Sprinkle the yeast over the water and let it sit for about 5-10 minutes, or until it becomes frothy.
3. Pour the yeast mixture into the dry ingredients and mix until a dough forms.
4. Knead the dough on a lightly floured surface for about 10 minutes, until smooth and elastic. You may need to add a bit more flour if the dough is too sticky.
5. Place the dough in a lightly greased bowl (use a bit of flour to dust instead of oil), cover with a damp cloth, and let it rise in a warm place for about 1 hour, or until doubled in size.
6. Punch down the dough and shape it into a loaf. Place it in a lightly greased loaf pan (again, use flour to dust if necessary).
7. Cover the loaf with a damp cloth and let it rise for another 30 minutes, or until doubled in size.
8. Preheat the oven to 375°F (190°C).
9. Bake the bread for 35-40 minutes, or until the crust is golden brown and the bread sounds hollow when tapped.
10. Remove the bread from the oven and let it cool on a wire rack before slicing.

When creating whole-grain bread, consider enhancing it with additional ingredients to elevate flavor, texture, and overall quality. These additions can transform a simple loaf into a delightful culinary experience. Happy baking!

Bread Enhancements

Vitamin C (Ascorbic Acid): Adding a pinch of vitamin C (ascorbic acid) to your dough can improve the bread's texture and help the yeast work better. It acts as a natural dough enhancer by strengthening gluten and promoting better rise.

Lemon Juice: Lemon juice adds acidity to the dough, which can enhance flavor and improve the overall quality of the bread. It also helps activate enzymes that contribute to better fermentation.

Dough Enhancer: Commercial dough enhancers often contain ingredients like lecithin, enzymes, and emulsifiers. These enhance dough elasticity, moisture retention, and shelf life. You can also make your own by combining ingredients like vital wheat gluten, lecithin, and ascorbic acid.

Vital Wheat Gluten: This protein-rich flour additive improves dough elasticity and structure. It's especially useful when working with whole grain flours, which tend to have less gluten.

Ground Flaxseed: Flaxseed adds a nutty flavor, fiber, and healthy fats to your bread. It also helps retain moisture and contributes to a softer crumb.

Ground Chia Seeds: Chia seeds absorb liquid and create a gel-like consistency, which helps keep the bread moist. They're also a great source of omega-3 fatty acids.

Potato Flakes: Potato flakes contribute to a soft, tender texture, retain moisture, and prevent the loaf from becoming too dry. They also add a subtle potato flavor and help delay staling, keeping your bread fresher longer.

Oat and Flaxseed Bread

Ingredients:

- 3 cups oat flour
- 1 cup whole wheat flour
- 2 tablespoons ground flaxseeds
- 2 1/4 teaspoons (1 packet) active dry yeast
- 1 1/2 teaspoons salt
- 2 tablespoons honey
- 1 1/2 cups warm water (110°F/45°C)

Instructions:

1. In a large mixing bowl, combine oat flour, whole wheat flour, ground flaxseeds, and salt.

2. In a small bowl, dissolve the honey in warm water. Sprinkle the yeast over the water and let it sit for about 5-10 minutes, or until it becomes frothy.

3. Pour the yeast mixture into the dry ingredients and mix until a dough forms.

4. Knead the dough on a lightly floured surface for about 10 minutes, until smooth and elastic. You may need to add a bit more flour if the dough is too sticky.

5. Place the dough in a lightly greased bowl (use a bit of flour to dust instead of oil), cover with a damp cloth, and let it rise in a warm place for about 1 hour, or until doubled in size.

6. Punch down the dough and shape it into a loaf. Place it in a lightly greased loaf pan (again, use flour to dust if necessary).

7. Cover the loaf with a damp cloth and let it rise for another 30 minutes, or until doubled in size.

8. Preheat the oven to 375°F (190°C).

9. Bake the bread for 35-40 minutes, or until the crust is golden brown and the bread sounds hollow when tapped.

10. Remove the bread from the oven and let it cool on a wire rack before slicing.

Honey Oat and Seed Bread

Ingredients:

- 3 cups oat flour
- 1 cup whole wheat flour
- 1/4 cup sunflower seeds
- 1/4 cup pumpkin seeds
- 2 1/4 teaspoons (1 packet) active dry yeast
- 1 1/2 teaspoons salt
- 2 tablespoons honey
- 1 1/2 cups warm water (110°F/45°C)

Instructions:

1. In a large mixing bowl, combine oat flour, whole wheat flour, sunflower seeds, pumpkin seeds, and salt.

2. In a small bowl, dissolve the honey in warm water. Sprinkle the yeast over the water and let it sit for about 5-10 minutes, or until it becomes frothy.

3. Pour the yeast mixture into the dry ingredients and mix until a dough forms.

4. Knead the dough on a lightly floured surface for about 10 minutes, until smooth and elastic. You may need to add a bit more flour if the dough is too sticky.

5. Place the dough in a lightly greased bowl (use a bit of flour to dust instead of oil), cover with a damp cloth, and let it rise in a warm place for about 1 hour, or until doubled in size.

6. Punch down the dough and shape it into a loaf. Place it in a lightly greased loaf pan (again, use flour to dust if necessary).

7. Cover the loaf with a damp cloth and let it rise for another 30 minutes, or until doubled in size.

8. Preheat the oven to 375°F (190°C).

9. Bake the bread for 35-40 minutes, or until the crust is golden brown and the bread sounds hollow when tapped.

10. Remove the bread from the oven and let it cool on a wire rack before slicing.

Add-In Suggestions:

- **Herbs and Spices:** Add dried herbs like rosemary, thyme, or basil for extra flavor. A pinch of cinnamon or nutmeg can add a warm, aromatic touch.

- **Grains:** Add cooked quinoa or millet to the dough for extra texture and nutrition.

- **Dried Fruit:** Add raisins, cranberries, or chopped dates for a touch of natural sweetness.

- **Nuts:** Add chopped walnuts, almonds, or pecans for a bit of crunch.

World War II Rationing: During World War II, oats were one of the few grains not rationed in many countries. They became a valuable food source during a time of scarcity and were used in various forms to supplement diets.

Quick Breads: Swift Delights

Banana Oat Bread

Ingredients:

- 2 cups oat flour
- 1 teaspoon baking soda
- 1/2 teaspoon salt
- 1 teaspoon cinnamon
- 3 ripe bananas, mashed
- 1/4 cup honey
- 1/4 cup unsweetened applesauce
- 1 teaspoon vanilla extract
- 1/2 cup chopped walnuts (optional)

Instructions:

1. Preheat the oven to 350°F (175°C). Grease a 9x5-inch (23x13 cm) loaf pan or line with parchment paper.

2. In a large bowl, mix oat flour, baking soda, salt, and cinnamon.

3. In another bowl, combine mashed bananas, honey, applesauce, and vanilla extract.

4. Add the wet ingredients to the dry ingredients and stir until just

combined. Fold in the chopped walnuts if using.

5. Pour the batter into the prepared loaf pan and smooth the top.

6. Bake for 50-60 minutes, or until a toothpick inserted into the center comes out clean.

7. Allow the bread to cool in the pan for 10 minutes before transferring to a wire rack to cool completely.

Pumpkin Oat Bread

Ingredients:

- 2 cups oat flour
- 1 teaspoon baking soda
- 1/2 teaspoon salt
- 1 teaspoon cinnamon
- 1/2 teaspoon nutmeg
- 1/2 teaspoon ginger
- 1 cup pumpkin puree
- 1/4 cup honey
- 1/4 cup unsweetened applesauce
- 1 teaspoon vanilla extract
- 1/2 cup chopped pecans (optional)

Instructions:

1. Preheat the oven to 350°F (175°C). Grease a 9x5-inch (23x13 cm) loaf pan or line with parchment paper.

2. In a large bowl, mix oat flour, baking soda, salt, cinnamon, nutmeg, and ginger.

3. In another bowl, combine pumpkin puree, honey, applesauce, and vanilla extract.

4. Add the wet ingredients to the dry ingredients and stir until just combined. Fold in the chopped pecans if using.

5. Pour the batter into the prepared loaf pan and smooth the top.

6. Bake for 50-60 minutes, or until a toothpick inserted into the center comes out clean.

7. Allow the bread to cool in the pan for 10 minutes before transferring to a wire rack to cool completely.

Lemon Poppy Seed Oat Bread

Ingredients:

- 2 cups oat flour
- 1 teaspoon baking soda
- 1/2 teaspoon salt
- 1 tablespoon poppy seeds
- 1/4 cup honey
- 1/4 cup unsweetened applesauce
- 1/2 cup lemon juice
- 1 teaspoon lemon zest
- 1 teaspoon vanilla extract

Instructions:

1. Preheat the oven to 350°F (175°C). Grease a 9x5-inch (23x13 cm) loaf pan or line with parchment paper.

2. In a large bowl, mix oat flour, baking soda, salt, and poppy seeds.

3. In another bowl, combine honey, applesauce, lemon juice, lemon zest, and vanilla extract.

4. Add the wet ingredients to the dry ingredients and stir until just combined.

5. Pour the batter into the prepared loaf pan and smooth the top.

6. Bake for 50-60 minutes, or until a toothpick inserted into the center comes out clean.

7. Allow the bread to cool in the pan for 10 minutes before transferring to a wire rack to cool completely.

Apple Cinnamon Oat Bread

Ingredients:

- 2 cups oat flour
- 1 teaspoon baking soda
- 1/2 teaspoon salt
- 1 teaspoon cinnamon
- 1/4 teaspoon nutmeg
- 1/4 cup honey
- 1/4 cup unsweetened applesauce
- 1 teaspoon vanilla extract
- 1 1/2 cups grated apples
- 1/2 cup chopped walnuts (optional)

Instructions:

1. Preheat the oven to 350°F (175°C). Grease a 9x5-inch (23x13 cm) loaf pan or line with parchment paper.

2. In a large bowl, mix oat flour, baking soda, salt, cinnamon, and nutmeg.

3. In another bowl, combine honey, applesauce, and vanilla extract.

4. Add the wet ingredients to the dry ingredients and stir until just combined. Fold in the grated apples and chopped walnuts if using.

5. Pour the batter into the prepared loaf pan and smooth the top.

6. Bake for 50-60 minutes, or until a toothpick inserted into the center comes out clean.

7. Allow the bread to cool in the pan for 10 minutes before removing.

Zucchini Oat Bread

Ingredients:

- 2 cups oat flour
- 1 teaspoon baking soda
- 1/2 teaspoon salt
- 1 teaspoon cinnamon
- 1/4 cup honey
- 1/4 cup unsweetened applesauce
- 1 teaspoon vanilla extract
- 1 1/2 cups grated zucchini
- 1/2 cup chopped walnuts (optional)

Instructions:

1. Preheat the oven to 350°F (175°C). Grease a 9x5-inch (23x13 cm) loaf pan or line with parchment paper.

2. In a large bowl, mix oat flour, baking soda, salt, and cinnamon.

3. In another bowl, combine honey, applesauce, and vanilla extract.

4. Add the wet ingredients to the dry ingredients and stir until just combined. Fold in the grated zucchini and chopped walnuts if using.

5. Pour the batter into the prepared loaf pan and smooth the top.

6. Bake for 50-60 minutes, or until a toothpick inserted into the center comes out clean.

7. Allow the bread to cool in the pan for 10 minutes before transferring to a wire rack to cool completely.

Chocolate Oat Bread

Ingredients:

- 2 cups oat flour
- 1/2 cup cocoa powder
- 1 teaspoon baking soda
- 1/2 teaspoon salt
- 1/4 cup honey
- 1/4 cup unsweetened applesauce
- 1 teaspoon vanilla extract
- 1 1/2 cups unsweetened almond milk
- 1/2 cup dairy-free chocolate chips (optional)

Instructions:

1. Preheat the oven to 350°F (175°C). Grease a 9x5-inch (23x13 cm) loaf pan or line with parchment paper.

2. In a large bowl, mix oat flour, cocoa powder, baking soda, and salt.

3. In another bowl, combine honey, applesauce, vanilla extract, and almond milk.

4. Add the wet ingredients to the dry ingredients and stir until just combined. Fold in the dairy-free chocolate chips if using.

5. Pour the batter into the prepared loaf pan and smooth the top.

6. Bake for 50-60 minutes, or until a toothpick inserted into the center comes out clean.

7. Allow the bread to cool in the pan for 10 minutes before transferring to a wire rack to cool completely.

Add-In Suggestions:

- **Dried Fruit:** Add raisins, cranberries, or chopped dates for extra sweetness.

- **Nuts and Seeds:** Add chopped nuts like walnuts, pecans, or seeds like chia and flaxseeds for added texture and nutrition.

- **Spices:** Experiment with spices like ginger, cardamom, or allspice to create different flavor profiles.

- **Extracts:** Vanilla, almond, or maple extracts can add a unique twist to your bread.

Enjoy these healthy, delicious oat flour breads!

Flippin' Fantastic: Oatmeal Pancakes Perfected

Flip out over our oatmeal pancakes that are so fluffy and flavorful, they'll make you leap out of bed with joy. These are not just pancakes; they're morning mood boosters, ready to stack up to your breakfast dreams!

Basic Oat Flour Pancakes

Ingredients:

- 1 cup oat flour

- 1 tsp baking powder

- 1/4 tsp sea salt

- 1 cup unsweetened oat milk (or any other plant-based milk)

- 1 tbsp apple cider vinegar (to create a buttermilk effect)

- 1/2 tsp vanilla extract (optional)

Instructions:

1. In a large bowl, mix the oat flour, baking powder, and salt together.

2. In a separate bowl, combine the oat milk and apple cider vinegar. Let it sit for a few minutes to curdle slightly.

3. Add the vanilla extract to the milk mixture (if using), then pour the wet ingredients into the dry ingredients.

4. Whisk until just combined; the batter should be slightly lumpy.

5. Heat a non-stick pan over medium heat. Pour 1/4 cup of batter for each pancake.

6. Cook until bubbles form on the surface, then flip and cook until golden brown on the other side.

Variations:

- **Banana Oat Pancakes:** Mash 1 ripe banana and add it to the batter for natural sweetness and moisture.

- **Blueberry Oat Pancakes:** Gently fold 1/2 cup of fresh or frozen blueberries into the batter for a fruity twist.

- **Cinnamon Spice Pancakes:** Add 1 tsp of cinnamon and a pinch of nutmeg to the dry ingredients for a warm, spiced flavor.

- **Chocolate Chip Oat Pancakes:** Mix in 1/4 cup of dark chocolate chips (look for sugar-free if avoiding sugar) into the batter for a decadent treat.

- **Savory Spinach Pancakes:** Incorporate 1/2 cup of finely chopped spinach and 1/4 cup of diced onions into the batter for a savory option.

Enjoy your healthy oat flour pancakes with your favorite sugar-free toppings like fresh fruit, nut butter, or a drizzle of sugar-free syrup!

Savory Oat Flour Pancakes with Herbs

Ingredients:

- 1 cup oat flour
- 1 tsp baking powder
- 1/2 tsp sea salt
- 1 cup unsweetened oat milk (or any plant-based milk)
- 1 tbsp apple cider vinegar
- 1/2 tsp dried Italian herbs (basil, oregano, thyme)
- 1/4 cup finely chopped scallions or chives
- Freshly ground black pepper to taste

Instructions:

1. In a mixing bowl, combine the oat flour, baking powder, salt, and dried herbs.

2. In a separate bowl, mix the oat milk and apple cider vinegar, and let it sit for a few minutes to create a buttermilk.

3. Pour the wet ingredients into the dry ingredients and stir until just combined.

4. Fold in the chopped scallions or chives and add black pepper to taste.

5. Heat a non-stick pan over medium heat and pour 1/4 cup of batter for each pancake.

6. Cook until bubbles appear on the surface, then flip and cook until golden brown on the other side.

Variations:

- **Zucchini Pancakes:** Add 1/2 cup of grated zucchini (excess moisture squeezed out) to the batter for added nutrition and moisture.

- **Corn and Jalapeño Pancakes:** Mix in 1/2 cup of corn kernels and 1 finely diced jalapeño for a spicy, sweet twist.

- **Tomato Basil Pancakes:** Incorporate 1/2 cup of diced tomatoes and extra basil into the batter for a Mediterranean flavor.

- **Cheesy Garlic Pancakes:** Add 1 tbsp of nutritional yeast and 1/2 tsp of garlic powder for a cheesy and garlicky taste.

Serve these savory pancakes with a dollop of sour cream or your favorite salsa for an extra kick. Enjoy your meal!

Oatcakes

Ingredients:

- 2 cups rolled oats (old-fashioned oats)

- 1 teaspoon baking powder

- 1/2 teaspoon salt

- 1 1/2 cups water

- Optional: additional seasonings like herbs, spices, or nutritional yeast for flavor (e.g., dried thyme, garlic powder, onion powder)

Instructions:

1. In a mixing bowl, combine the rolled oats, baking powder, salt, and any additional seasonings you'd like to add for flavor.

2. Gradually add the water to the dry ingredients, stirring until well combined. The mixture should have a thick, but pourable consistency. If it's too thick, add a little more water, until you reach the desired consistency.

3. Let the batter rest for about 5-10 minutes.

4. Heat a non-stick skillet or griddle over medium heat. Pour a ladleful of the oat batter onto the skillet, using the back of the ladle to spread it out into a thin, even circle.

5. Cook the oatcake for 2-3 minutes on one side, or until the edges start to look dry and bubbles form on the surface.

6. Carefully flip the oatcake using a spatula and cook for an additional 2-3 minutes on the other side, until golden brown and cooked through.

7. Serve the oatcakes warm with your choice of toppings, such as savory spreads, avocado, or sliced vegetables.

Serve for Oatcake Day (8th of August, in the UK) or any time you're craving a savory breakfast or snack!

Biscuit Bliss: Oatmeal's Wholesome Delight

Crisp, tender, and absolutely enchanting, these oatmeal biscuits are the ideal mates for your meal. Explore this chapter for a biscuit extravaganza that offers a satisfying snap with each morsel!

Basic Oat Flour Biscuits

Ingredients:

- 2 cups oat flour
- 1 tsp baking powder
- 1/2 tsp sea salt
- 3/4 cup cooked white beans, pureed
- 3/4 cup unsweetened oat milk (or any plant-based milk)

Instructions:

1. Preheat your oven to 375°F (190°C) and line a baking sheet with parchment paper.

2. In a large bowl, whisk together the oat flour, baking powder, and sea salt.

3. In a separate bowl, mix the pureed white beans with the oat milk until well combined.

4. Pour the wet mixture into the dry ingredients and stir until just combined. Be careful not to overmix.

5. Roll the dough to about 1 inch thick and use a biscuit cutter to cut out shapes. Or, drop spoonful of the dough onto the prepared baking sheet, spacing them about 2 inches apart.

6. Place the biscuits on a baking sheet lined with parchment paper.

7. Bake for 12-15 minutes, until the biscuits are lightly golden.

Variations:

- **Apple Cinnamon Biscuits:** Add 1/2 cup of finely diced apples and 1 tsp of cinnamon to the dough for a sweet, fruity flavor.

- **Savory Herb Biscuits:** Mix in 1 tbsp of dried Italian herbs and 1/4 tsp of garlic powder for a savory twist.

- **Pumpkin Spice Biscuits:** Incorporate 1/2 cup of pumpkin puree and 1 tsp of pumpkin pie spice into the dough for a fall-inspired treat.

- **Lemon Poppy Seed Biscuits:** Add the zest of one lemon and 1 tbsp of poppy seeds to the dough for a citrusy, crunchy variation.

These biscuits are versatile and can be enjoyed with a variety of toppings or as a side to your favorite meals. Enjoy experimenting with these recipes!

Oat Flour Biscuits

Ingredients:

- 2 cups oat flour

- 1 cup pureed white beans (cannellini or navy beans work well)

- 1 tsp baking powder

- 1/2 tsp sea salt

- 1/2 cup unsweetened applesauce (for moisture)

- Optional: 1 tsp dried herbs (like rosemary or thyme) for flavor

Instructions:

1. Preheat your oven to 375°F (190°C).

2. In a large bowl, mix the oat flour, baking powder, salt, and any optional dried herbs.

3. Stir in the pureed white beans and applesauce until well combined.

4. Place heaping spoonfulof the dough onto a parchment-lined baking sheet.

5. Flatten each spoonful slightly with the back of the spoon to form biscuit shapes.

6. Bake for 12-15 minutes, or until the biscuits are firm and lightly golden.

7. Let them cool on the baking sheet for a few minutes before transferring to a wire rack to cool completely.

Banana Oat Flour Biscuits

Ingredients:

- 2 cups oat flour

- 2 ripe bananas, mashed

- 1 tsp baking powder

- 1/2 tsp cinnamon

- 1/4 tsp nutmeg

- 1/2 tsp sea salt

- Optional: 1/4 cup raisins or chopped nuts for added texture

Instructions:

1. Preheat your oven to 375°F (190°C).

2. In a bowl, combine the oat flour, baking powder, cinnamon, nutmeg, and salt.

3. Add the mashed bananas (and raisins or nuts if using) to the dry ingredients and mix until a dough forms.

4. Proceed as with the white bean biscuits, dropping heaping spoonful of dough onto a baking sheet and flattening slightly.

5. Bake for 12-15 minutes, or until the edges are golden brown.

6. Allow to cool before serving.

"Cheesy" Oat Flour Biscuits (No Cheese)

Ingredients:

- 2 cups oat flour

- 1 cup mashed sweet potato (for moisture and natural sweetness)

- 1 tbsp nutritional yeast (for a cheesy flavor)

- 1 tsp baking powder

- 1/2 tsp garlic powder

- 1/2 tsp sea salt

- 1/4 cup water (or as needed)

Instructions:

1. Preheat your oven to 375°F (190°C).

2. In a large bowl, combine the oat flour, nutritional yeast, baking powder, garlic powder, and salt.

3. Add the mashed sweet potato to the dry ingredients and mix well.

4. Gradually add water until a dough forms. It should be moist but not sticky.

5. On a lightly floured surface, roll out the dough to about 1/2-inch thickness.

6. Use a biscuit cutter or a glass to cut out biscuit shapes and place them on a parchment-lined baking sheet.

7. Bake for 15-20 minutes, or until the biscuits are firm and slightly golden on the edges.

8. Let them cool on the baking sheet for a few minutes before transferring to a wire rack to cool completely.

Variations:

- **Herb and Onion Biscuits:** Add 1 tbsp of finely chopped fresh herbs (like parsley or chives) and 2 tbsp of finely minced onion to the dough for a flavorful twist.

- **Spicy Paprika Biscuits:** Mix in 1 tsp of smoked paprika into the dough for biscuits with a smoky, spicy kick.

Crisp Creations: Oat Crackers That Crack the Code

Discover the secret to the perfect crunch with oat crackers that are a cut above the rest.

Basic Oat Flour Crackers

Ingredients:

- 2 cups oat flour

- 1/2 tsp sea salt

- 1/2 cup water (add more if needed)

- Optional add-ins: sesame seeds, poppy seeds, dried herbs (like rosemary or thyme), garlic powder, or onion powder for flavor

Instructions:

1. Preheat your oven to 350°F (175°C).
2. In a large bowl, mix the oat flour and salt together (plus any dry add-ins).
3. Gradually add water and mix until a dough forms. It should be pliable but not sticky. Add more water, one tbsp at a time, if the dough is too dry.
4. Place the dough between two sheets of parchment paper and roll it out to your desired thickness.
5. Remove the top sheet of parchment and transfer the bottom sheet onto a baking sheet.
6. Use a knife or pizza cutter to score the dough into squares or rectangles.
7. Bake for 15-20 minutes or until the edges are lightly golden. Thicker crackers may take longer.

8. Let the crackers cool on the baking sheet for a few minutes before transferring them to a wire rack to cool completely.

Optional Toppings: Before baking, you can sprinkle the top of the dough with seeds like sesame or poppy seeds for extra flavor and crunch. Gently press them into the dough to adhere.

Mediterranean Herb Oat Flour Crackers

Ingredients:

- 2 cups oat flour
- 1 tsp dried oregano
- 1 tsp dried basil
- 1/2 tsp garlic powder
- 1/2 tsp onion powder
- 1/2 tsp sea salt
- 1/2 cup water (or as needed)
- Optional: 1 tbsp nutritional yeast for a cheesy flavor

Instructions:

1. Preheat your oven to 350°F (175°C).

2. In a mixing bowl, combine the dry ingredients, and nutritional yeast (if using).

3. Slowly add water to the dry ingredients, mixing until a cohesive dough forms. Add a little more water if the dough is too crumbly.

4. Place the dough on a piece of parchment paper and roll it out to about 1/8-inch thickness.

5. Cut the dough into squares or rectangles with a knife or pizza cutter.

6. Transfer the parchment paper with the dough onto a baking sheet.

7. Bake for 20-25 minutes, or until the crackers are crisp and golden brown around the edges.

8. Allow the crackers to cool on the baking sheet for 10 minutes before moving them to a cooling rack.

Serving Suggestion: Pair these herby crackers with a fresh Greek salad or dip them in hummus for a delightful snack.

Enjoy your homemade Mediterranean herb oat flour crackers, a tasty treat that's sure to please your palate!

Pizzazz in the Crust:
Oat Flour Pizza Crust

Elevate your pizza game with a crust that's not just a base but a taste sensation.

Basic Oat Pizza Crust

Ingredients:

- 2 cups oat flour
- 1 cup rolled oats
- 1/2 cup unsweetened oat milk (or any non-dairy milk)
- 1/2 tsp sea salt
- 1 tsp baking powder
- 1/2 tsp garlic powder (optional)
- 1/2 tsp dried oregano (optional)

Instructions:

1. Preheat your oven to 425°F (220°C) and line a baking sheet with parchment paper.
2. In a large bowl, combine the dry ingredients.
3. Gradually add oat milk, stirring until a dough forms. The dough should be slightly sticky but manageable.
4. Transfer the dough to the prepared baking sheet and press it into a round or rectangular shape about 1/4 inch thick.
5. Bake the crust for 15-20 minutes, or until lightly browned and firm to the touch.
6. Remove the crust from the oven and add your desired toppings.
7. Return the topped pizza to the oven and bake for an additional 10-15 minutes, or until the toppings are heated through and the edges of the crust are crispy.

Add-In Suggestions:

- Finely chopped fresh herbs like basil or parsley for added flavor.
- Ground flaxseeds or chia seeds for extra nutrition.
- A pinch of cumin or paprika for a savory twist.

Scottish Highland Games: The Scottish Highland Games often feature traditional Scottish dishes, many of which include oats. Visitors can enjoy oatcakes, porridge, and other oat-based treats while experiencing Scottish culture and athletics.

Spinach Oat Pizza Crust

Ingredients:

- 2 cups oat flour
- 1 cup rolled oats
- 1 cup fresh spinach, blended with water to make 1 cup of liquid
- 1/2 tsp sea salt
- 1 tsp baking powder
- 1/2 tsp garlic powder (optional)
- 1/2 tsp dried oregano (optional)

Instructions:

1. Preheat your oven to 425°F (220°C) and line a baking sheet with parchment paper.
2. In a large bowl, combine oat flour, rolled oats, salt, baking powder, garlic powder, and dried oregano.
3. Blend fresh spinach with water to make 1 cup of liquid.
4. Gradually add the spinach mixture to the dry ingredients, stirring until a dough forms.
5. Transfer the dough to the prepared baking sheet and press it into a round or rectangular shape about 1/4 inch thick.
6. Bake the crust for 15-20 minutes, or until lightly browned and firm to the touch.
7. Remove the crust from the oven and add your desired toppings.
8. Return the topped pizza to the oven and bake for an additional 10-15 minutes, or until the toppings are heated through and the edges of the crust are crispy.

Add-In Suggestions:

- Finely chopped fresh herbs like dill or parsley.
- Nutritional yeast for a cheesy flavor.
- Ground black pepper or red pepper flakes for a bit of heat.

Pizza Toppings:

- Tomato sauce, mushrooms, artichokes, black olives, red onions, and nutritional yeast.
- Cashew cream, broccoli, roasted red peppers, and cherry tomatoes.
- Hummus, roasted vegetables (like squash or sweet potatoes), and fresh spinach.

Carrot Oat Pizza Crust

Ingredients:

- 2 cups oat flour
- 1 cup rolled oats
- 1 cup finely grated carrots, blended with water to make 1 cup of liquid
- 1/2 tsp sea salt
- 1 tsp baking powder
- 1/2 tsp garlic powder (optional)
- 1/2 tsp dried oregano (optional)

Instructions:

1. Preheat your oven to 425°F (220°C) and line a baking sheet with parchment paper.

2. In a large bowl, combine oat flour, rolled oats, salt, baking powder, garlic powder, and dried oregano.

3. Blend finely grated carrots with water to make 1 cup of liquid.

4. Gradually add the carrot mixture to the dry ingredients, stirring until a dough forms.

5. Transfer the dough to the prepared baking sheet and press it into a round or rectangular shape about 1/4 inch thick.

6. Bake the crust for 15-20 minutes, or until lightly browned and firm to the touch.

7. Remove the crust from the oven and add your desired toppings.

8. Return the topped pizza to the oven and bake for an additional 10-15 minutes, or until the toppings are heated through and the edges of the crust are crispy.

Add-In Suggestions:

- Grated ginger for a zesty kick.
- Ground turmeric for an earthy flavor and vibrant color.
- Finely chopped cilantro or mint for freshness.

Pizza Toppings:

- Tomato sauce, spinach, mushrooms, bell peppers, and artichoke hearts.
- Cashew cheese, caramelized onions, roasted garlic, and fresh arugula.
- Pesto, cherry tomatoes, roasted eggplant, and capers.

Beet Oat Pizza Crust

Ingredients:

- 2 cups oat flour
- 1 cup rolled oats
- 1 cup finely grated beets, blended with water to make 1 cup of liquid
- 1/2 tsp sea salt
- 1 tsp baking powder
- 1/2 tsp garlic powder (optional)
- 1/2 tsp dried oregano (optional)

Instructions:

1. Preheat your oven to 425°F (220°C) and line a baking sheet with parchment paper.

2. In a large bowl, combine oat flour, rolled oats, salt, baking powder, garlic powder, and dried oregano.

3. Blend finely grated beets with water to make 1 cup of liquid.

4. Gradually add the beet mixture to the dry ingredients, stirring until a dough forms.

5. Transfer the dough to the prepared baking sheet and press it into a round or rectangular shape about 1/4 inch thick.

6. Bake the crust for 15-20 minutes, or until lightly browned and firm to the touch.

7. Remove the crust from the oven and add your desired toppings.

8. Return the topped pizza to the oven and bake for an additional 10-15 minutes, or until the toppings are heated through and the edges of the crust are crispy.

Add-In Suggestions:

- Ground coriander for a sweet, citrusy flavor.
- Crushed garlic for a pungent aroma.
- Lemon zest for a fresh, tangy note.

Instructions for Adding Pizza Toppings:

1. **Spread the Base:** Evenly spread your chosen base (tomato sauce, pesto, hummus, cashew cream, etc.) over the pre-baked crust.

2. **Add Toppings:**

3. **Bake Again:** Return the pizza to the oven and bake for 10-15 minutes, or until the toppings are heated through and the edges of the crust are crispy.

4. **Serve:** Let the pizza cool for a few minutes before slicing and serving.

Tortilla/Wrap Stars: Oat Flour's Take on the Perfect Package

Discover the dual-purpose delight of oat flour creations that serve as both wraps and tortillas. These recipes, crafted for wrap enthusiasts, are equally adept at taking on a tortilla's role. They're soft enough to fold without breaking, yet sturdy enough to hold a hearty filling. Whether you're in the mood for a traditional wrap or a taco-style treat, these oat flour wonders are your ticket to a world of flavorful possibilities. Bid farewell to the mundane and embrace the extraordinary versatility that awaits with every bite!

Basic Oat Wraps

Ingredients:

- 1 cup oat flour
- 1/2 cup whole wheat flour
- 1/2 tsp sea salt
- 1 cup water (more if needed)

Instructions:

1. In a large bowl, combine dry ingredients.
2. Gradually add water, stirring until a dough forms. The dough should be slightly sticky but manageable.
3. Knead the dough on a floured surface for about 5 minutes until smooth.
4. Divide the dough into 6-8 equal portions and roll each portion into a ball.
5. Roll each ball into a thin, round wrap on a floured surface.
6. Preheat a non-stick skillet over medium heat.
7. Cook each wrap for about 1-2 minutes on each side until lightly browned and cooked through.
8. Stack the cooked wraps and cover with a clean towel to keep them soft.

Add-In Suggestions:

- Fresh herbs (e.g., cilantro, parsley, basil)
- Ground flaxseeds or chia seeds for extra nutrition.
- A pinch of cumin or garlic powder for a savory twist.

Spinach Oat Wraps

Ingredients:

- 1 cup oat flour
- 1/2 cup whole wheat flour
- 1/2 tsp sea salt
- 1 cup fresh spinach, blended with water to make 1 cup of liquid

Instructions:

1. In a large bowl, combine oat flour, whole wheat flour, and salt.
2. Blend fresh spinach with water to make 1 cup of liquid.
3. Gradually add the spinach mixture to the dry ingredients, stirring until a dough forms.
4. Knead the dough on a floured surface for about 5 minutes until smooth.
5. Divide the dough into 6-8 equal portions and roll each portion into a ball.
6. Roll each ball into a thin, round wrap on a floured surface.
7. Preheat a non-stick skillet over medium heat.
8. Cook each wrap for about 1-2 minutes on each side until lightly browned and cooked through.
9. Stack the cooked wraps and cover with a clean towel to keep them soft.

Add-In Suggestions:

- Finely chopped herbs like dill or parsley.
- Nutritional yeast for a cheesy flavor.
- Ground black pepper or red pepper flakes for a bit of heat.

Carrot Oat Wraps

Ingredients:

- 1 cup oat flour
- 1/2 cup whole wheat flour
- 1/2 tsp sea salt
- 1 cup finely grated carrots, blended with water to make 1 cup of liquid

Instructions:

1. In a large bowl, combine oat flour, whole wheat flour, and salt.
2. Blend finely grated carrots with water to make 1 cup of liquid.

3. Gradually add the carrot mixture to the dry ingredients, stirring until a dough forms.

4. Knead the dough on a floured surface for about 5 minutes until smooth.

5. Divide the dough into 6-8 equal portions and roll each portion into a ball.

6. Roll each ball into a thin, round wrap on a floured surface.

7. Preheat a non-stick skillet over medium heat.

8. Cook each wrap for about 1-2 minutes on each side until lightly browned and cooked through.

9. Stack the cooked wraps and cover with a clean towel to keep them soft.

Add-In Suggestions:

- Grated ginger for a zesty kick.

- Ground turmeric for an earthy flavor and vibrant color.

- Finely chopped cilantro or mint for freshness.

Beet Oat Wraps

Ingredients:

- 1 cup oat flour

- 1/2 cup whole wheat flour

- 1/2 tsp sea salt

- 1 cup finely grated beets, blended with water to make 1 cup of liquid

Instructions:

1. In a large bowl, combine oat flour, whole wheat flour, and salt.

2. Blend finely grated beets with water to make 1 cup of liquid.

3. Gradually add the beet mixture to the dry ingredients, stirring until a dough forms.

4. Knead the dough on a floured surface for about 5 minutes until smooth.

5. Divide the dough into 6-8 equal portions and roll each portion into a ball.

6. Roll each ball into a thin, round wrap on a floured surface.

7. Preheat a non-stick skillet over medium heat.

8. Cook each wrap for about 1-2 minutes on each side until lightly browned and cooked through.

9. Stack the cooked wraps and cover with a clean towel to keep them soft.

Add-In Suggestions:

- Ground coriander for a sweet, citrusy flavor.

- Crushed garlic for a pungent aroma.

- Lemon zest for a fresh, tangy note.

Tips for Storing and Using Oat Wraps:

- **Storage:** Store the cooked wraps in an airtight container or plastic bag at room temperature for up to 2 days. For longer storage, refrigerate for up to 5 days or freeze for up to a month. To reheat, wrap them in a damp paper towel and microwave for 15-20 seconds.

- **Using Wraps:** These wraps are versatile and can be filled with a variety of fillings, such as hummus and vegetables, avocado and beans, or tofu scramble. They also work well as a base for quesadillas or even as a pizza crust substitute.

Health Food Movement: Oats experienced a resurgence in popularity during the late 20th century with the rise of the health food movement. Their high fiber content and cholesterol-lowering properties led to increased consumption and the development of oat-based products like granola bars and oat milk.

What did the oat say when it won the race?

I'm oat-standing in my field!

Muffin Magic: Oat Flour's Marvelous Morsels

Muffins get a makeover with oat flour, turning them into moist, tender treats that are sure to disappear as soon as they're out of the oven!

Apple Cinnamon Oat Muffins

Ingredients:

- 1 1/2 cups oat flour
- 1 cup unsweetened applesauce
- 1 cup whole wheat flour
- 1/2 cup unsweetened oat milk (or any non-dairy milk)
- 1/2 cup finely chopped dates
- 1/2 cup finely chopped apples
- 2 tbsp ground flaxseed mixed with 6 tbsp water (flax egg)
- 2 tsp baking powder
- 1 tsp ground cinnamon
- 1/2 tsp baking soda
- 1/2 tsp vanilla extract
- 1/4 tsp sea salt
- 1/4 tsp ground nutmeg

Instructions:

1. Preheat your oven to 350°F (175°C) and line a muffin tin with paper liners.

2. In a large bowl, combine the oat flour, whole wheat flour, baking powder, baking soda, cinnamon, nutmeg, and salt.

3. In another bowl, mix the applesauce, flaxseed, oat milk, vanilla extract, dates, and chopped apples.

4. Add the wet ingredients to the dry ingredients and stir until just combined.

5. Spoon the batter into the muffin tin, filling each cup about 3/4 full.

6. Bake for 20-25 minutes, or until a toothpick inserted into the center of a muffin comes out clean.

7. Allow to cool in the tin for a few minutes before transferring to a wire rack to cool completely.

Blueberry Banana Oat Muffins

Ingredients:

- 1 1/2 cups oat flour
- 1 cup mashed ripe bananas (about 2 large bananas)
- 1 cup whole wheat flour
- 1/2 cup unsweetened oat milk (or any non-dairy milk)
- 1/2 cup fresh or frozen blueberries
- 1/4 cup date sugar (optional)
- 2 tbsp ground flaxseed mixed with 6 tbsp water (flax egg)
- 2 tsp baking powder
- 1 tsp ground cinnamon
- 1/2 tsp baking soda
- 1/2 tsp vanilla extract
- 1/4 tsp sea salt

Instructions:

1. Preheat your oven to 350°F (175°C) and line a muffin tin with paper liners.

2. In a large bowl, combine the oat flour, whole wheat flour, baking powder, baking soda, cinnamon, and salt.

3. In another bowl, mix the mashed bananas, flaxseed, oat milk, vanilla extract, and date sugar (if using).

4. Add the wet ingredients to the dry ingredients and stir until just combined.

5. Gently fold in the blueberries.

6. Spoon the batter into the muffin tin, filling each cup about 3/4 full.

7. Bake for 20-25 minutes, or until a toothpick inserted into the center of a muffin comes out clean.

8. Allow to cool in the tin for a few minutes before transferring to a wire rack to cool completely.

National Oatmeal Day (USA): National Oatmeal Day is celebrated annually on October 29th in the United States. While it's not a festival in the traditional sense, it's a day dedicated to promoting the nutritional benefits and versatility of oatmeal. Many people celebrate by enjoying oatmeal-based dishes and sharing oatmeal recipes.

Carrot Raisin Oat Muffins

Ingredients:

- 1 1/2 cups oat flour
- 1 cup grated carrots
- 1 cup whole wheat flour
- 1/2 cup unsweetened applesauce
- 1/2 cup unsweetened oat milk (or any non-dairy milk)
- 1/2 cup raisins
- 1/4 cup date sugar (optional)
- 2 tbsp ground flaxseed mixed with 6 tbsp water (flax egg)
- 2 tsp baking powder
- 1 tsp ground cinnamon
- 1/2 tsp baking soda
- 1/2 tsp vanilla extract
- 1/4 tsp ground ginger
- 1/4 tsp sea salt

Instructions:

1. Preheat your oven to 350°F (175°C) and line a muffin tin with paper liners.
2. In a large bowl, combine the oat flour, whole wheat flour, flaxseed, baking powder, baking soda, cinnamon, ginger, and salt.
3. In another bowl, mix the grated carrots, flaxseed, applesauce, oat milk, vanilla extract, and date sugar (if using).
4. Add the wet ingredients to the dry ingredients and stir until just combined.
5. Fold in the raisins.
6. Spoon the batter into the muffin tin, filling each cup about 3/4 full.
7. Bake for 20-25 minutes, or until a toothpick inserted into the center of a muffin comes out clean.
8. Allow to cool in the tin for a few minutes before transferring to a wire rack to cool completely.

> **Oat Fest (Canada):** Oat Fest is an annual event held in Ontario, Canada, celebrating all things oats. The festival features oat-themed activities, workshops, and food vendors serving up creative oat-based dishes. It's a fun and educational event for oat lovers of all ages.

Chocolate Banana Oat Muffins

Ingredients:

- 1 1/2 cups oat flour
- 1 cup mashed ripe bananas (about 2 large bananas)
- 1 cup whole wheat flour
- 1/2 cup unsweetened oat milk (or any non-dairy milk)
- 1/4 cup cocoa powder
- 1/4 cup date sugar (optional)
- 2 tbsp ground flaxseed mixed with 6 tbsp water (flax egg)
- 2 tsp baking powder
- 1/2 tsp baking soda
- 1/2 tsp vanilla extract
- 1/4 tsp sea salt

Instructions:

1. Preheat your oven to 350°F (175°C) and line a muffin tin with paper liners.

2. In a large bowl, combine the oat flour, whole wheat flour, cocoa powder, baking powder, baking soda, and salt.

3. In another bowl, mix the mashed bananas, flaxseed, oat milk, vanilla extract, and date sugar (if using).

4. Add the wet ingredients to the dry ingredients and stir until just combined.

5. Spoon the batter into the muffin tin, filling each cup about 3/4 full.

6. Bake for 20-25 minutes, or until a toothpick inserted into the center of a muffin comes out clean.

7. Allow to cool in the tin for a few minutes before transferring to a wire rack to cool completely.

> Why did the chocolate banana oat muffin apply for a job at the bank?
>
> Because it wanted to help others "raise" their dough!

Pumpkin Spice Oat Muffins

Ingredients:

- 1 1/2 cups oat flour
- 1 cup canned pumpkin puree
- 1 cup whole wheat flour
- 1/2 cup unsweetened oat milk (or any non-dairy milk)
- 1/4 cup date sugar (optional)
- 2 tbsp ground flaxseed mixed with 6 tbsp water (flax egg)
- 2 tsp baking powder
- 1 tsp ground cinnamon
- 1/2 tsp ground ginger
- 1/2 tsp ground nutmeg
- 1/2 tsp baking soda
- 1/2 tsp vanilla extract
- 1/4 tsp ground cloves
- 1/4 tsp sea salt

Instructions:

1. Preheat your oven to 350°F (175°C) and line a muffin tin with paper liners.
2. In a large bowl, combine the oat flour, whole wheat flour, baking powder, baking soda, cinnamon, ginger, nutmeg, cloves, and salt.
3. In another bowl, mix the pumpkin puree, oat milk, flaxseed, vanilla extract, and date sugar (if using).
4. Add the wet ingredients to the dry ingredients and stir until just combined.
5. Spoon the batter into the muffin tin, filling each cup about 3/4 full.
6. Bake for 20-25 minutes, or until a toothpick inserted into the center of a muffin comes out clean.
7. Allow to cool in the tin for a few minutes before transferring to a wire rack to cool completely.

These muffins are wholesome and delicious. Enjoy them as a healthy breakfast or snack!

> Why did the muffin go to the doctor?
>
> It felt a little "crumby" and needed some "sweet" attention!

Apple Cinnamon Oat Muffins with Streusel Topping

Ingredients:

Muffins:

- 1 1/2 cups oat flour
- 1 cup unsweetened applesauce
- 1 cup whole wheat flour
- 1/2 cup unsweetened oat milk (or any non-dairy milk)
- 1/2 cup finely chopped dates
- 1/2 cup finely chopped apples
- 2 tbsp ground flaxseed mixed with 6 tbsp water (flax egg)
- 2 tsp baking powder
- 1 tsp ground cinnamon
- 1/2 tsp baking soda
- 1/2 tsp vanilla extract
- 1/4 tsp sea salt
- 1/4 tsp ground nutmeg

Streusel Topping:

- 1/2 cup rolled oats
- 1/4 cup oat flour
- 1/4 cup finely chopped nuts (optional)
- 2 tbsp date sugar (optional)
- 1 tsp ground cinnamon
- 1/4 cup unsweetened applesauce

Instructions:

1. Preheat your oven to 350°F (175°C) and line a muffin tin with paper liners.

2. In a large bowl, combine the dry ingredients.

3. In another bowl, mix the wet ingredients.

4. Add the wet ingredients to the dry ingredients and stir until just combined.

5. Spoon the batter into the muffin tin, filling each cup about 3/4 full.

6. To make the streusel topping, mix all ingredients in a small bowl.

7. Sprinkle the streusel topping evenly over the muffins.

8. Bake for 20-25 minutes, or until a toothpick inserted into the center of a muffin comes out clean.

9. Allow to cool in the tin for a few minutes before transferring to a wire rack to cool completely.

Blueberry Banana Oat Muffins with Streusel Topping

Ingredients:

Muffins:

- 1 1/2 cups oat flour
- 1 cup mashed ripe bananas (about 2 large bananas)
- 1 cup whole wheat flour
- 1/2 cup unsweetened oat milk (or any non-dairy milk)
- 2 tbsp ground flaxseed mixed with 6 tbsp water (flax egg)
- 1/2 cup fresh or frozen blueberries
- 1/4 cup date sugar (optional)
- 2 tsp baking powder
- 1 tsp ground cinnamon
- 1/2 tsp baking soda
- 1/2 tsp vanilla extract
- 1/4 tsp sea salt

Streusel Topping:

- 1/2 cup rolled oats
- 1/4 cup oat flour
- 1/4 cup finely chopped nuts (optional)
- 2 tbsp date sugar (optional)
- 1 tsp ground cinnamon
- 1/4 cup unsweetened applesauce

Instructions:

1. Preheat your oven to 350°F (175°C) and line a muffin tin with paper liners.
2. In a large bowl, combine the oat flour, whole wheat flour, baking powder, baking soda, cinnamon, and salt.
3. In another bowl, mix the wet ingredients.
4. Add the wet ingredients to the dry ingredients and stir until just combined.
5. Gently fold in the blueberries.
6. Spoon the batter into the muffin tin, filling each cup about 3/4 full.
7. To make the streusel topping, mix all ingredients in a small bowl.
8. Sprinkle the streusel topping evenly over the muffins.
9. Bake for 20-25 minutes, or until a toothpick inserted into the center of a muffin comes out clean.
10. Allow to cool for a few minutes before transferring to a wire rack.

Carrot Raisin Oat Muffins with Streusel Topping

Ingredients:

Muffins:

- 1 1/2 cups oat flour
- 1 cup grated carrots
- 1 cup whole wheat flour
- 1/2 cup unsweetened applesauce
- 1/2 cup unsweetened oat milk (or any non-dairy milk)
- 2 tbsp ground flaxseed mixed with 6 tbsp water (flax egg)
- 1/2 cup raisins
- 1/4 cup date sugar (optional)
- 2 tsp baking powder
- 1 tsp ground cinnamon
- 1/2 tsp baking soda
- 1/2 tsp vanilla extract
- 1/4 tsp ground ginger
- 1/4 tsp sea salt

Streusel Topping:

- 1/2 cup rolled oats
- 1/4 cup oat flour
- 1/4 cup finely chopped nuts (optional)
- 2 tbsp date sugar (optional)
- 1 tsp ground cinnamon
- 1/4 cup unsweetened applesauce

Instructions:

1. Preheat your oven to 350°F (175°C) and line a muffin tin with paper liners.

2. In a large bowl, combine the dry ingredients.

3. In another bowl, mix the wet ingredients.

4. Add the wet ingredients to the dry ingredients and stir until just combined.

5. Fold in the raisins.

6. Spoon the batter into the muffin tin, filling each cup about 3/4 full.

7. To make the streusel topping, mix all ingredients in a small bowl.

8. Sprinkle the streusel topping evenly over the muffins.

9. Bake for 20-25 minutes, or until a toothpick inserted into the center of a muffin comes out clean.

10. Allow to cool for a few minutes before transferring to a wire rack.

Chocolate Banana Oat Muffins with Streusel Topping

Ingredients:

Muffins:

- 1 1/2 cups oat flour

- 1 cup mashed ripe bananas (about 2 large bananas)

- 1 cup whole wheat flour

- 1/2 cup unsweetened oat milk (or any non-dairy milk)

- 2 tbsp ground flaxseed mixed with 6 tbsp water (flax egg)

- 1/4 cup cocoa powder

- 1/4 cup date sugar (optional)

- 2 tsp baking powder

- 1/2 tsp baking soda

- 1/2 tsp vanilla extract

- 1/4 tsp sea salt

Streusel Topping:

- 1/2 cup rolled oats

- 1/4 cup oat flour

- 1/4 cup finely chopped nuts (optional)

- 2 tbsp date sugar (optional)

- 1 tsp ground cinnamon

- 1/4 cup unsweetened applesauce

Instructions:

1. Preheat your oven to 350°F (175°C) and line a muffin tin with paper liners.

2. In a large bowl, combine the oat flour, whole wheat flour, cocoa powder, baking powder, baking soda, and salt.

3. In another bowl, mix the mashed bananas, oat milk, flaxseed, vanilla extract, and date sugar (if using).

4. Add the wet ingredients to the dry ingredients and stir until just combined.

5. Spoon the batter into the muffin tin, filling each cup about 3/4 full.

6. To make the streusel topping, mix all ingredients in a small bowl.

7. Sprinkle the streusel topping evenly over the muffins.

8. Bake for 20-25 minutes, or until a toothpick inserted into the center of a muffin comes out clean.

9. Allow to cool in the tin for a few minutes before transferring to a wire rack to cool completely.

Pumpkin Spice Muffins

Ingredients:

Muffins:

- 1 1/2 cups oat flour
- 1 cup canned pumpkin puree
- 1 cup whole wheat flour
- 1/2 cup unsweetened oat milk (or any non-dairy milk)
- 1/4 cup date sugar (optional)
- 2 tbsp ground flaxseed mixed with 6 tbsp water (flax egg)
- 2 tsp baking powder
- 1 1/2 tsp ground cinnamon
- 1/2 tsp ground ginger
- 1/2 tsp ground nutmeg
- 1/2 tsp baking soda
- 1 tsp vanilla extract
- 1/4 tsp ground cloves
- 1/4 tsp sea salt

Streusel Topping:

- 1/2 cup rolled oats
- 1/4 cup oat flour
- 1/4 cup finely chopped nuts
- 2 tbsp date sugar
- 1 tsp ground cinnamon
- 1/4 cup unsweetened applesauce

Instructions:

1. Preheat your oven to 350°F (175°C) and line a muffin tin with paper liners.

2. In a large bowl, combine the dry ingredients.

3. In another bowl, mix the wet ingredients.

4. Add the wet ingredients to the dry ingredients and stir until just combined.

5. Spoon the batter into the muffin tin, filling each cup about 3/4 full.

6. To make the streusel topping, mix the rolled oats, oat flour, nuts (if using), date sugar (if using), cinnamon, and applesauce in a small bowl.

7. Sprinkle the streusel topping evenly over the muffins.

8. Bake for 20-25 minutes, or until a toothpick inserted into the center of a muffin comes out clean.

9. Allow to cool in the tin for a few minutes before transferring to a wire rack to cool completely.

Chapter 11: Sweet Oat-asis: A Haven of Oat Delights

Embark on a delectable journey through the oasis of oat-infused sweetness! This chapter is a treasure trove of treats that will make your heart and taste buds sing. From the energizing zing of Oatmeal Energy Balls to the comforting embrace of Oat Bars, each recipe is a testament to the versatility of oats. Indulge in the classic charm of Oat Cookies, or let the innovative Pie Crusts surprise you with their wholesome goodness. The Streusel Topping will add a crumbly crown to your creations, while the Brownies promise a rich, guilt-free indulgence. Prepare to fall in love with every spoonful of these heavenly oatmeal desserts!

Oatmeal Energy Balls: Bites of Vigor

Jumpstart your day with these little spheres of joy! Packed with flavor and energy, these Oatmeal Energy Balls are your go-to snack for a quick pick-me-up.

Date and Almond Energy Balls

Ingredients:

- 1 cup rolled oats
- 1 cup pitted dates
- 1/2 cup almonds
- 1/4 cup unsweetened applesauce
- 1 tsp vanilla extract
- 1/2 tsp ground cinnamon

Instructions:

1. Place the rolled oats, dates, almonds, applesauce, vanilla extract, and cinnamon in a food processor.

2. Process until the mixture is well combined and starts to come together.

3. Roll the mixture into small balls (about 1 inch in diameter).

4. Place the energy balls on a baking sheet lined with parchment paper.

5. Refrigerate for at least 1 hour to set.

6. Store in an airtight container in the refrigerator for up to a week.

Banana Oat Energy Balls

Ingredients:

- 1 cup rolled oats
- 1 ripe banana, mashed
- 1/4 cup unsweetened shredded coconut
- 1/4 cup raisins
- 1 tsp vanilla extract
- 1/2 tsp ground cinnamon

Instructions:

1. In a large bowl, combine the mashed banana, oats, shredded coconut, raisins, vanilla extract, and cinnamon.
2. Mix until well combined.
3. Roll the mixture into small balls (about 1 inch in diameter).
4. Place the energy balls on a baking sheet lined with parchment paper.
5. Refrigerate for at least 1 hour to set.
6. Store in an airtight container in the refrigerator for up to a week.

Apple Cinnamon Energy Balls

Ingredients:

- 1 cup rolled oats
- 1/2 cup unsweetened applesauce
- 1/4 cup chopped dried apples (unsweetened)
- 1/4 cup chopped walnuts (optional)
- 1 tsp ground cinnamon
- 1/2 tsp vanilla extract

Instructions:

1. In a large bowl, combine the oats, applesauce, dried apples, walnuts (if using), cinnamon, and vanilla extract.
2. Mix until well combined.
3. Roll the mixture into small balls (about 1 inch in diameter).
4. Place the energy balls on a baking sheet lined with parchment paper.
5. Refrigerate for at least 1 hour to set.
6. Store in an airtight container in the refrigerator for up to a week.

Blueberry Oat Energy Balls

Ingredients:

- 1 cup rolled oats
- 1/2 cup unsweetened dried blueberries
- 1/4 cup unsweetened applesauce
- 1/4 cup ground flaxseed
- 1 tsp vanilla extract
- 1/2 tsp ground cinnamon

Instructions:

1. In a large bowl, combine the oats, dried blueberries, applesauce, ground flaxseed, vanilla extract, and cinnamon.
2. Mix until well combined.
3. Roll the mixture into small balls (about 1 inch in diameter).
4. Place the energy balls on a baking sheet lined with parchment paper.
5. Refrigerate for at least 1 hour to set.
6. Store in an airtight container in the refrigerator for up to a week.

Carrot Cake Energy Balls

Ingredients:

- 1 cup rolled oats
- 1/2 cup grated carrots
- 1/4 cup raisins
- 1/4 cup unsweetened applesauce
- 1 tsp vanilla extract
- 1 tsp ground cinnamon
- 1/2 tsp ground nutmeg

Instructions:

1. In a large bowl, combine the oats, grated carrots, raisins, applesauce, vanilla extract, cinnamon, and nutmeg.
2. Mix until well combined.
3. Roll the mixture into small balls (about 1 inch in diameter).
4. Place the energy balls on a baking sheet lined with parchment paper.
5. Refrigerate for at least 1 hour to set.
6. Store in an airtight container in the refrigerator for up to a week.

These energy balls are packed with natural ingredients, providing a healthy and convenient snack option. Enjoy!

Oat Bars: Layers of Love

Discover the layered delight of Oat Bars, where every bite is a harmonious blend of texture and taste. Perfect for on-the-go indulgence or a leisurely treat.

Banana Oat Bars

Ingredients:

- 3 ripe bananas, mashed
- 2 cups rolled oats
- 1/2 cup chopped dates
- 1 flax egg (1 tbsp ground flaxseed mixed with 3 tbsp water)
- 1/4 cup unsweetened shredded coconut
- 1 tsp cinnamon
- 1/4 tsp sea salt

Instructions:

1. Preheat your oven to 350°F (175°C).
2. In a large bowl, mix all the ingredients.
3. Press the mixture firmly into a lined 8x8-inch baking pan.
4. Bake for 25-30 minutes or until the edges are golden brown.
5. Let the bars cool in the pan before cutting into squares.

Apple Cinnamon Oat Flour Bars

Ingredients:

- 2 cups oat flour
- 1 cup unsweetened applesauce
- 1 flax egg (1 tbsp ground flaxseed mixed with 3 tbsp water)
- 1/2 cup raisins
- 1/2 cup finely chopped apple
- 1 tsp cinnamon
- 1/2 tsp nutmeg
- 1/4 tsp sea salt

Instructions:

1. Preheat your oven to 350°F (175°C).
2. Combine all ingredients in a bowl and mix until well incorporated.
3. Press the dough evenly into a lined 8x8-inch baking pan.
4. Bake for 20-25 minutes or until firm and the edges start to turn golden.
5. Allow to cool before slicing into bars.

Pumpkin Spice Oat Bars

Ingredients:

- 2 cups rolled oats
- 1 cup pumpkin puree (not pumpkin pie filling)
- 1 flax egg (1 tbsp ground flaxseed mixed with 3 tbsp water)
- 1/4 cup pureed dates
- 1 tsp pumpkin pie spice
- 1/4 tsp sea salt

Instructions:

1. Preheat your oven to 350°F (175°C).
2. In a large bowl, mix all the ingredients.
3. Spread the mixture into a lined 8x8-inch baking pan, pressing down firmly.
4. Bake for 25-30 minutes or until set and the edges are lightly browned.
5. Cool completely before cutting into bars.

These recipes are naturally sweetened with fruits making them a healthier option for a snack or breakfast.

Cherry Almond Oat Bars

Ingredients:

- 2 cups rolled oats
- 1/2 cup almond butter
- 1/2 cup chopped dried cherries
- 1 flax egg (1 tbsp ground flaxseed mixed with 3 tbsp water)
- 1/2 tsp cinnamon or nutmeg (optional)
- 2-3 tbsp maple syrup or honey (optional)
- 1/4 cup sliced almonds
- 1 tsp almond extract
- 1/4 tsp sea salt

Instructions:

1. Preheat your oven to 350°F (175°C).
2. In a bowl, mix all the ingredients until well combined.
3. Firmly press the mixture into a lined 8x8-inch baking pan.
4. Bake for 20-25 minutes or until the bars are firm and the edges are slightly brown.
5. Let them cool before cutting into bars.

Oat Cookies: Crispy Companions

Crisp on the edges and chewy in the middle, these Oat Cookies are the perfect companions for your lunch, after-school snack or a cozy night in.

Oatmeal Fruit and Nut Cookies

Ingredients:

- 2 cups rolled oats
- 1 ripe banana, mashed
- 1/2 cup unsweetened applesauce
- 1/4 cup raisins
- 1/4 cup dried cranberries or chopped dates
- 1/4 cup chopped walnuts or almonds
- 1 flax egg (1 tbsp ground flaxseed mixed with 3 tbsp water)
- 1/4 tsp nutmeg or ginger (optional)
- 2-3 tbsp maple syrup or honey (optional)
- 1 tsp cinnamon
- 1/2 tsp vanilla extract
- A pinch of sea salt (optional)

Instructions:

1. Preheat your oven to 350°F (175°C).
2. In a small bowl, mix 1 tablespoon of ground flaxseed with 3 tablespoons of water. Let it sit for a few minutes to thicken.
3. In a large bowl, mix the mashed banana, applesauce, rolled oats, raisins, dried cranberries or dates, chopped nuts, cinnamon, vanilla extract, sea salt, flax egg, and any optional spices or sweeteners until well combined.
4. Drop spoonful of the mixture onto a lined baking sheet.
5. Bake for 15-20 minutes or until the edges are golden brown.
6. Let them cool before serving.

What did the oatmeal cookie say to the raisin?

You're the raisin for my existence!

Banana Oat Cookies

Ingredients:

- 2 ripe bananas, mashed
- 1 cup rolled oats
- 1/2 cup raisins or chopped dates
- 1 flax egg (1 tbsp ground flaxseed mixed with 3 tbsp water)
- 1/4 tsp ginger (optional)
- 2-3 tbsp maple syrup or honey (optional)
- 1/2 tsp cinnamon
- 1/4 tsp nutmeg

Instructions:

1. Preheat your oven to 350°F (175°C).
2. In a bowl, mix the mashed bananas and rolled oats raisins or chopped dates, cinnamon, and nutmeg, flax egg and any optional spices or sweeteners until well combined.
3. Place heaping spoonful of the mixture onto a baking sheet lined with parchment paper.
4. Flatten each cookie slightly with the back of the spoon.
5. Bake for 15-18 minutes or until the edges are golden brown.
6. Let them cool before serving.

Chickpea Chocolate Chip Cookies

Ingredients:

- 1 can (15 oz) chickpeas, drained and rinsed
- 1 cup rolled oats
- 1/2 cup unsweetened applesauce
- 1 flax egg (1 tbsp ground flaxseed mixed with 3 tbsp water)
- 1/4 cup pureed dates
- 1 tsp vanilla extract
- 1/2 tsp baking soda
- A pinch of sea salt
- 1/2 cup dark chocolate chips

Instructions:

1. Preheat oven to 350°F (175°C).
2. In a food processor, blend the ingredients except chocolate chips until smooth.
3. Stir in the chocolate chips by hand.
4. Place heaping spoonful of the dough onto a baking sheet lined with parchment paper.
5. Bake for 20-25 minutes or until set and lightly browned. Allow to cool before serving.

Apple Cinnamon Oat Cookies

Ingredients:

- 1 cup rolled oats
- 1/2 cup unsweetened applesauce
- 1/4 cup finely chopped apple
- 1 flax egg (1 tbsp ground flaxseed mixed with 3 tbsp water)
- 1/4 cup chopped walnuts (optional)
- 1 tsp ground cinnamon
- 1/4 tsp ground ginger

Instructions:

1. Preheat your oven to 350°F (175°C).
2. In a bowl, combine all ingredients and mix until well incorporated.
3. Spoon the mixture onto a baking sheet lined with parchment paper, forming cookie shapes.
4. Bake for 18-22 minutes or until the cookies are firm and the edges are slightly browned.
5. Let them cool on the baking sheet before transferring to a wire rack.

Pumpkin Oat Cookies

Ingredients:

- 1 cup rolled oats
- 1/2 cup pumpkin puree (not pumpkin pie filling)
- 1 flax egg (1 tbsp ground flaxseed mixed with 3 tbsp water)
- 1/4 cup pureed dates
- 1 tsp pumpkin pie spice
- 1/4 tsp sea salt
- Optional: pumpkin seeds for topping

Instructions:

1. Preheat your oven to 350°F (175°C).
2. In a bowl, mix all ingredients until well combined.
3. Place heaping spoonful of the mixture onto a baking sheet lined with parchment paper.
4. Press a few pumpkin seeds on top of each cookie if desired.
5. Bake for 15-20 minutes or until the cookies are firm and the edges start to brown.
6. Cool on the baking sheet before transferring to a wire rack.

No-Bake Chocolate Oat Cookies

Ingredients:

1 cup rolled oats

1/2 cup unsweetened cocoa powder

1/2 cup mashed ripe bananas

1/4 cup chopped dates

1/4 cup nut butter (almond, peanut, or cashew)

1 tsp vanilla extract

Optional: 1/4 cup shredded coconut

Instructions:

In a large bowl, mix the cocoa powder and rolled oats.

Add the mashed bananas, chopped dates, nut butter, vanilla extract, and optional shredded coconut. Stir until all ingredients are well combined and the mixture is sticky.

Line a baking sheet with parchment paper.

Place heaping spoonful of the mixture onto the baking sheet and flatten if desired.

Chill in the refrigerator for at least 30 minutes before serving.

No-Bake Blondie Oat Cookies

Ingredients:

- 1 cup rolled oats
- 1/2 cup unsweetened shredded coconut
- 1/2 cup mashed ripe bananas
- 1/4 cup finely chopped apples
- 1/4 cup raisins or dried cranberries
- 1 tsp cinnamon

Instructions:

1. In a large bowl, combine the rolled oats and shredded coconut.

2. Add the mashed bananas, chopped apples, raisins or dried cranberries, and cinnamon. Mix until everything is well incorporated.

3. Line a baking sheet with parchment paper.

4. Spoon the mixture onto the baking sheet, forming cookie shapes.

5. Refrigerate for at least 30 minutes to set the cookies before enjoying.

Oatmeal Date Sugar Cookies

Ingredients:

- 1 1/2 cups rolled oats, ground into flour
- 1 cup pitted dates, soaked in warm water
- 1 flax egg (1 tbsp ground flaxseed mixed with 3 tbsp water)
- 1 ripe banana, mashed
- 1 tsp vanilla extract
- 1/4 tsp baking soda
- A pinch of sea salt

Instructions:

1. Preheat your oven to 350°F (175°C).
2. Drain the dates and blend them in a food processor until they form a smooth paste.
3. Add the rest of the ingredients and pulse until well combined.
4. Line a baking sheet with parchment paper.
5. Place heaping spoonful of the dough onto the sheet and flatten them into cookie shapes.
6. Bake for 12-15 minutes or until the edges are golden brown.
7. Allow the cookies to cool on the baking sheet before transferring to a wire rack.

Banana Oat Shortbread Cookies

Ingredients:

- 2 cups rolled oats, ground into flour
- 2 ripe bananas, mashed
- 1/4 cup unsweetened applesauce
- 1 tsp almond extract (or vanilla extract)
- A pinch of sea salt

Instructions:

1. Preheat your oven to 350°F (175°C).
2. In a large bowl, combine the oat flour, mashed bananas, applesauce, almond extract, and salt. Stir until a dough forms.
3. Place the dough between two sheets of parchment paper and roll out to about 1/4-inch thickness.

4. Use a cookie cutter to cut out shapes and place them on a baking sheet lined with parchment paper.

5. Bake for 15-20 minutes or until the cookies are firm and the edges are slightly golden.

6. Let the cookies cool completely before serving.

Peanut Butter Oat Cookies

Ingredients:

- 1 cup oat flour (you can make your own by blending rolled oats)

- 1/2 cup peanut butter

- 1 flax egg (1 tbsp ground flaxseed mixed with 3 tbsp water)

- 1/4 cup maple syrup or agave nectar (for sweetness)

- 1 teaspoon vanilla extract

- 1/4 teaspoon baking soda

- A pinch of salt (optional, or use miso for a salty twist)

- Dairy-free chocolate chips (optional, for extra indulgence)

-

Instructions:

1. Preheat your oven to 350°F (180°C) and line a baking sheet with parchment paper.

2. In a mixing bowl, combine oat flour, peanut butter, maple syrup (or agave), flax egg,

3. vanilla extract, baking soda, and salt (if using). Mix until well combined.

4. If the dough seems too sticky, chill it in the refrigerator for 10-15 minutes.

5. Scoop out small portions of dough (about 1 tablespoon each) and roll them into balls. Place them on the prepared baking sheet.

6. Flatten each ball slightly with a fork, creating a crisscross pattern.

7. Bake for 10-12 minutes or until the edges are golden brown.

8. Let the cookies cool on the baking sheet for a few minutes before transferring them to a wire rack to cool completely.

Enjoy these wholesome peanut butter oat cookies as a snack, dessert, or even breakfast! Feel free to customize by adding chopped nuts, dried fruit, or extra spices.

The Cake Walk

Vanilla Whisper Cake

Ingredients:

- 2 cups oat flour
- 1 tsp baking powder
- 1/2 tsp baking soda
- 1/4 tsp salt
- 1 cup oat milk
- 1/2 cup mashed bananas
- 1/4 cup unsweetened applesauce
- 1 tbsp vinegar (apple cider or white distilled) mixed with 1 tsp baking soda
- 1 tsp vanilla extract

Instructions:

1. Preheat your oven to 350°F (175°C).
2. In a bowl, sift the dry ingredients.
3. In another bowl, mix wet ingredients.
4. Combine the wet and dry ingredients until just mixed. Pour into a greased 8x8 inch (20x20 cm) or a 9-inch (23 cm) round cake pan and bake for 25-30 minutes or until a toothpick comes out clean.

Simply Sweet Cocoa Cake

Ingredients:

- 1 1/2 cups oat flour
- 1 cup pitted Medjool dates, soaked in boiling water and pureed
- 1/4 cup unsweetened cocoa powder
- 1 teaspoon baking soda
- 1/2 teaspoon sea salt
- 1 cup water
- 1 teaspoon distilled white vinegar
- 1 teaspoon vanilla extract

Instructions:

1. Preheat your oven to 350°F (175°C).
2. In a greased 8x8 inch (20x20 cm) or a 9-inch (23 cm) round cake pan, put in all the dry ingredients and stir.
3. In a bowl mix all the wet ingredients.
4. Make a well in the dry ingredients. Pour in the wet ingredients.
5. Stir until just combined.

6. Bake for about 30 minutes or until a toothpick inserted into the center comes out clean.

7. Allow to cool before serving.

Tropical Twist Carrot Cake

Ingredients:

- 2 cups oat flour
- 1 tsp baking soda
- 1/2 tsp salt
- 1 tsp cinnamon
- 1/2 tsp nutmeg
- 1/4 tsp allspice
- 1 cup grated carrots
- 1 cup crushed pineapple (drained)
- 1/2 cup shredded coconut
- 1/2 cup chopped walnuts or pecans
- 1 cup unsweetened applesauce
- 1 flax egg (1 tbsp ground flaxseed mixed with 3 tbsp water) or for a lighter texture (1 tbsp vinegar (apple cider or white distilled) mixed with 1 tsp baking soda)
- 1/2 cup maple syrup
- 1 tsp vanilla extract

Instructions:

1. Preheat your oven to 350°F (175°C) and grease a 9-inch cake pan.

2. In a large bowl, whisk together the oat flour, baking soda, salt, cinnamon, nutmeg, and allspice.

3. In another bowl, mix the grated carrots, crushed pineapple, shredded coconut, and chopped nuts.

4. Add the applesauce, maple syrup, flax egg, and vanilla extract to the dry ingredients and mix until just combined.

5. Fold in the carrot mixture until well incorporated.

6. Pour the batter into the prepared cake pan and smooth the top with a spatula.

7. Bake for 30-35 minutes or until a toothpick inserted into the center comes out clean.

8. Allow the cake to cool in the pan for 10 minutes before transferring it to a wire rack to cool completely.

Enjoy your homemade carrot cake with a tropical twist!

Pie Crusts: The Oat Couture

Elevate your pies with these chic Oat Pie Crusts that offer a rustic charm and a heartier, healthier base for your favorite fillings. Not the pie crusts you are used to.

Oat Flour Pie Crust

Ingredients:

- 1 1/2 cups oat flour (made from ground rolled oats)
- 1/4 tsp sea salt
- 1/4 cup unsweetened applesauce
- 1/2 tsp white vinegar
- 2-3 tbsp cold water

Instructions:

1. Preheat your oven to 375°F (190°C).
2. In a mixing bowl, combine the oat flour and salt.
3. Add the applesauce and vinegar. Mix until a crumbly dough forms.
4. Gradually add cold water, one tbsp at a time, until the dough comes together. Be careful not to overmix.
5. Shape the dough into a ball and flatten it slightly.
6. Roll out the dough between two sheets of parchment paper to fit your pie dish.
7. Carefully transfer the rolled-out crust to the pie dish and press it into place.
8. Trim any excess dough hanging over the edges.
9. Use a fork to prick the bottom of the crust to prevent it from puffing up during baking.
10. Bake the crust for 10-12 minutes or until lightly golden.
11. Let it cool before filling with your favorite pie filling.

This oat flour crust is nutty, tender, and perfect for both sweet and savory pies.

> What's an oat's favorite pickup line?
>
> Are you a bowl of oatmeal? Because you're warming my heart!

Date-Sweetened Oat Pie Crust

Ingredients:

- 1 1/2 cups rolled oats
- 1 cup pitted dates, soaked in warm water for 10 minutes
- 1/4 cup water (use the soaking water for extra sweetness)
- 1 tsp ground cinnamon
- 1/2 tsp white vinegar
- 1/4 tsp sea salt

Instructions:

1. Preheat your oven to 375°F (190°C).
2. Drain the dates and reserve the soaking water.
3. In a food processor, grind the rolled oats into a fine flour.
4. Add the soaked dates, water, cinnamon, vinegar, and salt to the food processor with the oat flour. Blend until the mixture forms a sticky dough.
5. Press the dough evenly into the bottom and up the sides of a pie dish.
6. Bake for 15-20 minutes or until the crust is firm and lightly browned.
7. Allow the crust to cool before filling with your pie filling of choice.

This crust is naturally sweet and a chewy base that complements a variety of fillings, especially fruit or custard.

Why did the oatmeal go to therapy?

Because they were feeling cereal-ly stressed out!

Banana Oat Pie Crust

Ingredients:

- 2 cups rolled oats
- 2 ripe bananas, mashed
- 1 tsp ground cinnamon
- 1/4 tsp sea salt
- 1/2 tsp white vinegar
- 1/2 cup chopped nuts (such as walnuts, pecans, or almonds)

Instructions:

1. Preheat your oven to 375°F (190°C).
2. In a food processor, pulse the rolled oats until they resemble a coarse flour.
3. In a mixing bowl, combine the oat flour with the mashed bananas, cinnamon, vinegar, and salt. Mix until a dough forms.
4. Stir in the chopped nuts.
5. Press the dough into the bottom and up the sides of a pie dish.
6. Bake for 15-20 minutes or until the edges are golden brown.
7. Allow the crust to cool before filling with preferred pie filling.

Apple Oat Pie Crust

Ingredients:

- 2 cups rolled oats
- 1/2 cup unsweetened applesauce
- 1 tsp vanilla extract
- 1/2 tsp ground cinnamon
- 1/4 tsp sea salt

Instructions:

1. Preheat your oven to 375°F (190°C).
2. Grind the rolled oats in a food processor until you get a fine oat flour.
3. Combine the oat flour with applesauce, vanilla extract, cinnamon, and salt in a bowl. Stir until well combined and a dough forms.
4. Press the mixture into a pie dish, forming an even layer on the bottom and sides.
5. Bake for 15-20 minutes or until the crust is firm and slightly golden.
6. Let the crust cool completely before adding your pie filling.

Streusel Topping: The Oat Crown

Sprinkle a bit of magic on your desserts with this Oat Streusel Topping, adding a delightful crunch and a touch of elegance to any sweet dish.

Oat Streusel Topping

Ingredients:

- 1 cup rolled oats
- 1/2 cup chopped nuts (such as almonds, walnuts, or pecans)
- 1/4 cup date paste (made by blending soaked dates with a bit of water)
- 1 tsp ground cinnamon
- 1/4 tsp ground nutmeg
- 1/4 tsp sea salt
- 2 tbsp unsweetened applesauce

Instructions:

1. Preheat your oven to 350°F (175°C).
2. In a bowl, combine the rolled oats, chopped nuts, date paste, cinnamon, nutmeg, and salt. Mix well.
3. Add the applesauce to the mixture and stir until everything is well coated and clumpy.
4. Spread the mixture on a baking sheet lined with parchment paper.
5. Bake for 10-15 minutes, stirring occasionally, until the topping is golden brown and crispy.
6. Let it cool before using it to top your favorite desserts.

This streusel topping is perfect for adding a crunchy texture to fruit crisps, muffins, or yogurt without the need for added sugars.

Enjoy your healthy and delicious creation!

Why don't you ever argue with a Streusel Topping?

Because it's always right on top of the argument, and it's got a crumbly disposition!

Brownies: The Oat Fudge Factor

Savor the rich and gooey goodness of these Oat Brownies, where indulgence meets wholesome oats for a guilt-free chocolate experience.

Fudgy Black Bean Oat Brownies

Ingredients:

1 can (15 oz) black beans, drained and rinsed

2 cups pitted dates

1 flax egg (1 tbsp ground flaxseed mixed with 3 tbsp water)

1/2 cup rolled oats

1/2 cup unsweetened cocoa powder

1/4 cup unsweetened applesauce

1 tsp vanilla extract

1/2 tsp baking powder

A pinch of sea salt
Optional: walnuts or dark chocolate chips

Instructions:

1. Preheat your oven to 350°F (175°C) and line an 8-inch (20 cm) square baking pan with parchment paper.
2. In a food processor, blend the oats into a fine flour.
3. Add the black beans, dates, cocoa powder, applesauce, flax egg, vanilla extract, baking powder, and salt to the food processor. Blend until smooth.
4. If using, fold in walnuts or chocolate chips.
5. Spread the batter evenly in the prepared pan.
6. Bake for 20-25 minutes or until a toothpick inserted into the center comes out clean.
7. Let the brownies cool completely before cutting into squares.

What's an oat's favorite type of music?

Oat-pera!

Sweet Potato Chocolate Brownies

Ingredients:

- 2 medium sweet potatoes, peeled and steamed
- 1 cup pitted dates, soaked in warm water
- 1 cup rolled oats, ground into flour
- 1/2 cup unsweetened cocoa powder
- 1/2 cup oat milk
- 1 flax egg (1 tbsp ground flaxseed mixed with 3 tbsp water)
- 1 tsp vanilla extract
- 1/2 tsp baking soda
- A pinch of sea salt
- Optional: chopped nuts or chocolate chips

Instructions:

1. Preheat your oven to 350°F (175°C) and line an 8-inch (20 cm) square baking pan with parchment paper.

2. Blend the steamed sweet potatoes and soaked dates in a food processor until smooth.

3. Add the flax egg and dry ingredients. Blend until well combined.

4. If desired, stir in nuts or chocolate chips.

5. Pour the batter into the prepared pan and smooth the top with a spatula.

6. Bake for 25-30 minutes or until a toothpick inserted into the center comes out mostly clean.

7. Let the brownies cool in the pan before cutting into squares.

Brownie Creation Legend: One popular story is that of a famous Chicago socialite, who in 1893 requested a pastry chef at the Palmer House Hotel to create a dessert for ladies attending the Chicago World's Columbian Exposition. The Palmer House Brownie was made with chocolate with walnuts and apricot glaze.

Why did the Brownie apply for a job? Because it wanted to prove it could bring a lot to the "table" and wasn't just another "crumby" dessert!

Chickpea Chocolate Brownies

Ingredients:

- 1 can (15 oz) chickpeas, drained and rinsed
- 1 cup pitted dates, soaked in warm water
- 1/2 cup rolled oats, ground into flour
- 1/3 cup unsweetened cocoa powder
- 1/4 cup unsweetened applesauce
- 1 flax egg (1 tbsp ground flaxseed mixed with 3 tbsp water)
- 1/4 cup pure maple syrup
- 1 tsp baking powder
- A pinch of sea salt
- Optional: sugar-free chocolate chips or cacao nibs

Instructions:

1. Preheat your oven to 350°F (175°C) and line an 8-inch (20 cm) square baking pan with parchment paper.

2. In a food processor, blend the chickpeas and soaked dates until smooth.

3. Add the dry ingredients and flax egg. Process until the mixture is smooth.

4. If using, fold in chocolate chips or cacao nibs.

5. Spread the batter evenly in the prepared pan.

6. Bake for 20-25 minutes or until the edges start pulling away from the pan's sides.

7. Allow the brownies to cool before cutting into squares.

> **First Known Recipe:** The first known recipe for brownie, a dessert made with molasses cakes, appeared in the 1896 version of the Boston Cooking-School Cook Book by Fannie Farmer.

> Why did the Chickpea Chocolate Brownie refuse to play hide and seek? Because it knew that, no matter where it hid, it would always be "bean" found delicious!

Zucchini Oat Chocolate Brownies

Ingredients:

- 2 cups grated zucchini (excess water squeezed out)
- 1 cup pitted dates, soaked in warm water
- 1 cup rolled oats, ground into flour
- 1/2 cup unsweetened cocoa powder
- 1/4 cup unsweetened applesauce
- 1 flax egg (1 tbsp ground flaxseed mixed with 3 tbsp water)
- 1/4 cup pure maple syrup
- 1 tsp vanilla extract
- 1/2 tsp baking powder
- A pinch of sea salt
- Optional: walnuts or chocolate chips

Instructions:

1. Preheat your oven to 350°F (175°C) and line an 8-inch (20 cm) square baking pan with parchment paper.

2. In a food processor, blend the soaked dates until they form a paste.

3. Add the grated zucchini, oat flour, cocoa powder, applesauce, flax egg, maple syrup, vanilla extract, baking powder, and salt. Blend until combined.

4. If desired, stir in walnuts or chocolate chips.

5. Pour the batter into the prepared pan and smooth the top with a spatula.

6. Bake for 30-35 minutes or until a toothpick inserted into the center comes out clean.

7. Let the brownies cool before cutting into squares.

Why did the Zucchini Oat Chocolate Brownie avoid the gym? Because it didn't want to "squash" its soft, delicious texture!

Banana Oat Blondies

Ingredients:

- 3 ripe bananas, mashed
- 2 cups rolled oats
- 1/2 cup date sugar or finely chopped dates
- 1/4 cup almond butter or peanut butter
- 1 flax egg (1 tbsp ground flaxseed mixed with 3 tbsp water)
- 1 tsp vanilla extract
- 1/2 tsp baking powder
- A pinch of cinnamon (optional)
- A pinch of sea salt
- 3/4 cup of chopped nuts (such as walnuts, almonds, or pecans) (optional)

Instructions:

1. Preheat your oven to 350°F (175°C) and line an 8-inch (20 cm) square baking pan with parchment paper.
2. Grind oats into a fine flour.
3. In a large bowl, mix the mashed bananas with the date sugar, almond butter, flax egg, vanilla extract, baking powder, cinnamon, and salt.
4. Stir in the oat flour until well combined.
5. Stir in nuts if using.
6. Spread the mixture evenly in the prepared pan.
7. Bake for 25-30 minutes or until the edges are golden brown and a toothpick inserted into the center comes out clean.
8. Allow the blondies to cool before cutting into squares.

Why did the Banana Oat Blondie go to school? Because it wanted to be a "smart cookie" and improve its "batter" understanding!

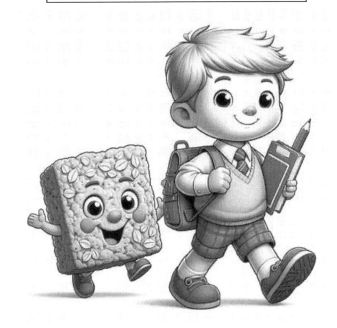

Chapter 12: Oatstanding Versatility: Beyond the Bowl

Unleash the full potential of oats that takes you into a world of oat-based creativity. From pampering your skin to greening your garden, discover how this humble grain can do it all!

Beauty and Skincare: Oat Couture: Radiance Recipes

Step into the oat couture of skincare with recipes that will leave you glowing in this spa-worthy section.

Oatmeal Face Mask

Ingredients:

- 1/3 cup rolled oats (These provide gentle exfoliation and soothe the skin)

- 1/2 cup hot water (not boiling)

- 1 tbsp honey (Honey is moisturizing and has antibacterial properties)

- 1-2 tbsp yogurt (optional for extra moisture)

Instructions:

1. Grind the oats in a food processor until they become a fine powder.

2. Mix the ground oats with hot water and let them sit for a few minutes to form a paste.

3. Stir in the honey and yogurt until well combined.

4. Apply the mask to your face, avoiding the eye area.

5. Leave on for 10-15 minutes, then rinse with warm water.

Banana Oat Face Mask

Ingredients:

- 1 ripe banana
- 2 tablespoons rolled oats
- 1 teaspoon honey

Instructions:

1. Mash the banana until smooth.
2. Mix in the rolled oats and honey.
3. Apply the mask to your face and leave it on for 15-20 minutes.
4. Rinse off with warm water.

Avocado Oat Face Mask

Ingredients:

- 1/2 ripe avocado
- 2 tablespoons oat flour (you can make this by blending rolled oats)
- 1 teaspoon plain yogurt

Instructions:

1. Mash the avocado until creamy.
2. Add oat flour and yogurt, mixing well.
3. Apply the mask and relax for 15 minutes.
4. Rinse off gently.

Aromatherapy Infusions: Incorporating Essential Oils

Essential oils can enhance your face masks, but it's essential to use them in moderation. Here are some options:

Lavender Oil: Known for its calming properties, lavender oil can soothe the skin. Add 1-2 drops to your mask.

Tea Tree Oil: With antibacterial properties, tea tree oil can be helpful for acne-prone skin. Use 1 drop.

Frankincense Oil: Frankincense is rejuvenating and may promote healthy skin. Add 1 drop.

Chamomile Oil: Chamomile is gentle and soothing. Use 1-2 drops.

Rosehip Oil: Rich in vitamins, rosehip oil can nourish the skin. Add 1-2 drops.

Remember to do a patch test first to ensure you don't have any adverse reactions. Enjoy your spa-like experience!

Oat Eye Compress

Soothe tired eyes:

A cup of cooled chamomile tea.

Soak a clean cloth in the tea, then sprinkle with rolled oats.

Place the cloth over your closed eyes for a few minutes.

Oat Lip Scrub

For soft, kissable lips:

Mix 1 tbsp ground oats with 1 tsp brown sugar.

Add a few drops of olive oil or coconut oil.

Gently scrub your lips to remove dead skin.

Oatmeal Body Scrub

Ingredients:

- 1/2 cup rolled oats
- 1/4 cup brown sugar
- 1/4 cup oil (coconut, almond, or olive oil)
- Optional: essential oils for fragrance

Instructions:

1. Pulse the oats in a food processor to a coarse texture.
2. Mix the oats with brown sugar and oil until it forms a scrub consistency.
3. If desired, add a few drops of essential oil.
4. Use the scrub on damp skin, gently massaging in a circular motion.
5. Rinse off in the shower and pat dry.

Soothing Oat Bath

Ingredients:

- 1 cup rolled oats
- A muslin cloth or an old stocking

Instructions:

1. Place the oats in the muslin cloth or stocking and tie it closed.
2. Drop the oat-filled cloth into a warm bath.
3. Soak in the bath, using the oat bag as a gentle sponge.

Oat Bath Bombs

Create soothing oat bath bombs by combining:

- 1 cup baking soda
- 1/2 cup citric acid
- 1/2 cup cornstarch
- 1/2 cup ground oats
- A few drops of your favorite essential oil
- Witch hazel (spray bottle)

Mix the dry ingredients, add the essential oil, and spritz with witch hazel until the mixture holds together. Shape into balls and let them dry. Drop one into your bath for a relaxing soak.

Oat Hair Mask

Revitalize your hair with an oat-based mask:

Blend 1/2 cup rolled oats with 1/2 cup warm water until smooth.

Add a tbsp of honey and mix well.

Apply to damp hair, leave for 20 minutes, then rinse thoroughly.

Oatmeal Hand Soak

Ingredients:

- 1/4 cup rolled oats
- Warm water
- A few drops of Frankincense Oil (optional)
- A few drops of Lavender Oil (optional)

Instructions:

1. Fill a bowl with warm water and add the oats.

2. Soak your hands for 10-15 minutes to soften the skin and soothe irritation.

Oat Hand Softener

For silky-smooth hands:

Mix equal parts ground oats and coconut oil.

A few drops of Sandalwood Oil (optional)

Massage into your hands, focusing on dry areas.

Rinse off with warm water.

Notes: Remember, oats are gentle and suitable for most skin types. Customize these ideas to fit your preferences, and enjoy the natural benefits of oats in your beauty routine!

These natural oat-based beauty treatments can help nourish and revitalize your skin.

Remember to do a patch test before applying any new product to your skin to ensure you don't have an allergic reaction. Enjoy pampering yourself with these oat-inspired skincare delights!

Roman Oat Consumption: The Romans were known to have cultivated oats as a food crop. They primarily used oats as livestock feed, but they also consumed them themselves, often in the form of porridge.

Household Uses:
Oat & About: Clever Home Concoctions

Oats aren't just for eating; they're for living! Get ready for some ingenious oat-infused solutions that will revolutionize your household routine.

Natural Deodorizer: Oats can absorb odors. Place a bowl of dry oats in your refrigerator or any musty space to neutralize unpleasant smells.

Eco-Friendly Cleaning Scrub: Ground oats can be used as a gentle cleaning scrub for surfaces. Just sprinkle some on the surface and scrub away with a damp cloth.

Oat Bath Bags: Fill a small cloth bag with oats and tie it securely. You can use this as a soothing bath scrub or drop it in the bathwater for a skin-softening soak.

Carpet Freshener: Mix ground oats with baking soda and a few drops of essential oil. Sprinkle the mixture on your carpet, let it sit for a few minutes, then vacuum it up for a fresh scent.

Plant Watering Helper: If you tend to overwater plants, adding a layer of oats to the bottom of the pot can help absorb excess water and protect the roots from rot.

Dry Shampoo: Ground oats can be used as a dry shampoo for pets or even humans. Rub some into the hair, then brush it out to absorb oils and freshen up between washes.

Doorstop Sachet: Create a sachet filled with oats and dried lavender to use as a doorstop. It will hold the door and release a pleasant aroma when moved.

Drawer Freshener: Similar to the deodorizer, a sachet of oats can keep drawers smelling fresh. You can also add dried herbs or flowers for an extra scent boost.

Oatmeal Sachets for Laundry: Add a sachet of oats to your laundry to help soften fabrics naturally. It's especially good for delicate items that could benefit from a gentle touch.

Oat Pillow Filler: Use whole oats as a natural pillow filler. They can provide a comfortable, breathable alternative to traditional stuffing and may offer a gentle, soothing scent to help with relaxation and sleep.

Note: These oat-based hacks are not only practical but also environmentally friendly. Enjoy trying them out in your home!

Crafts and DIY Projects:
The Art of Oats:
Crafty Creations

Dive into the artful world of oats where grains become your canvas. These DIY projects will turn oats into masterpieces of crafty ingenuity.

Oatmeal Play Dough

I have had this recipe for years and do not know where it originated.

Ingredients:

- 2.5 cups water
- 1 1/4 cup salt
- 1 1/2 tablespoons cream of tartar
- 5 tablespoons vegetable oil
- 2.5 cups flour (all-purpose or wheat flour)
- Food coloring or liquid watercolors (for vibrant hues)

instructions:

1. In a large pot, combine water, salt, cream of tartar, and vegetable oil.
2. Mix well until somewhat smooth.
3. Add the flour to the pot and continue stirring until fully combined.
4. If you want colored playdough, mix food coloring or liquid watercolors into the water before adding it to the dry ingredients.
5. Cook the mixture over low-medium heat, stirring continuously, until it forms a smooth, pliable dough.
6. Remove from heat and let it cool.
7. Knead the playdough until it reaches the desired consistency.
8. Store in a sealed container or bag to keep it fresh for months.

Scented Oatmeal Play Dough

Add a sensory experience by incorporating natural scents. Here's how:

Ingredients:

- 1 cup rolled oats
- 1/2 cup flour
- 1/2 cup water
- Essential oils (like lavender, orange, or peppermint)

Instructions:

1. Grind the oats in a food processor until they have a fine texture.
2. In a bowl, mix the ground oats with flour and water until a dough forms.
3. If you want colored dough, divide the dough into portions and knead in a few drops of food coloring into each.
4. Now your oatmeal play dough is ready for sculpting!

Note: Remember, while the play dough is non-toxic.

Oat and Honey Soap

Ingredients:

- Melt and pour soap base
- 1/4 cup rolled oats
- Honey
- Soap molds

Instructions:

1. Cut the soap base into chunks and melt in a double boiler.
2. Once melted, stir in the oats and a few tbsp of honey.
3. Pour the mixture into soap molds and let it set until hard.

Oatmeal Lavender Sachets

Ingredients:

- Dried lavender flowers
- Rolled oats
- Small cloth bags or squares of fabric

Instructions:

1. Mix equal parts of dried lavender and oats.
2. Fill the bags or fabric squares with the mixture and tie them closed.
3. Place the sachets in drawers or hang in closets.

Oat-Based Bird Feeder

Ingredients:

- Rolled oats
- Peanut butter
- Birdseed
- Pine cones or toilet paper rolls

Instructions:

1. Coat the pine cones or toilet paper rolls in peanut butter.
2. Roll them in oats and then in birdseed.
3. Hang them outside on tree branches for the birds to enjoy.

The Oatdoor Garden: Thriving Thickets

Let oats take root in your garden with tips and tricks for using them to nurture your green space. It's all about growing green with grains.

Oat Mulch: Oats can be used as mulch to protect plants, retain moisture, and suppress weeds. Simply sprinkle dry oat flakes around the base of your plants.

Seed Starting Mix: Create a nutritious seed starting mix by combining: 2 parts soil, 1 part oat flakes, 1 part compost

Mix well and use it to fill your seed trays.

Oat Tea Fertilizer: Brew a batch of oat tea to use as a mild fertilizer for your plants.

1 cup rolled oats to 1 gallon of water

Soak the oats in the water for 24 hours.

Strain the oats and use the water to water your plants.

Oat-Based Plant Pot: Create biodegradable plant pots using a mixture of oat flour and water. Mold them into the desired shape and let them dry. Plant your seedlings in them, and when ready, you can plant the whole pot in the garden.

Oatmeal Worm Food: If you have a worm composting bin, oats are a great food source for the worms. Just sprinkle some on top of the compost as a treat.

Note: Always use plain, unflavored oats for gardening purposes to avoid any additives that might harm your plants. These are just a few ways you can incorporate oats into your gardening routine. Enjoy your green endeavors!

> What did the oat say when it won the gardening competition? "I'm feeling grain-tastic!"

> How do oats stay in shape? They always do their "crunches" in the garden!

> Why did the oat go to the garden party? Because it was a cereal entertainer!

Pet Care: Oat Pawsibilities: Tail-Wagging Treats

Discover the paw-sibilities of oats in pet care with treats that will have tails wagging and pets purring. Wholesome and hearty, these oat delights are pet-approved.

Oatmeal Delight for Dogs

Ingredients:

- 1 cup rolled oats
- 2 cups water
- 1 mashed banana
- 1/4 cup blueberries
- 1/4 cup diced apple (no seeds)

Instructions:

1. In a saucepan, bring the water to a boil.
2. Add the rolled oats and simmer for about 10 minutes until the oats are soft.
3. Remove from heat and let it cool down to room temperature.
4. Stir in the mashed banana, blueberries, and diced apple.
5. Serve in small portions suitable for your dog's size.

Oat Dog Biscuits

Ingredients:

- 2 cups rolled oats
- 1/2 cup unsweetened applesauce
- 1/4 cup unsweetened peanut butter (make sure it's xylitol-free)
- 1/4 cup vegetable broth or water

Instructions:

1. Preheat your oven to 350°F (175°C).
2. In a blender or food processor, grind the rolled oats into a fine flour.
3. In a large bowl, mix the oat flour with the applesauce, peanut butter, and vegetable broth until a dough forms.
4. Roll out the dough on a floured surface to about 1/4 inch thick.
5. Use a cookie cutter to cut out biscuit shapes and place them on a baking sheet lined with parchment paper.
6. Bake for 25-30 minutes or until the biscuits are golden brown and firm.
7. Let them cool completely before serving to your dog.

Quick Oat and Banana Dog Treats

Ingredients:

- 1 cup rolled oats

- 1/2 ripe banana, mashed

- 2 tablespoons water

Instructions:

1. Preheat oven to 350°F (175°C).

2. Mix all ingredients in a bowl until well combined.

3. Form into small balls and flatten on a baking sheet.

4. Bake for 15 minutes or until edges are golden.

5. Cool before serving.

Tip: For a special touch, add a drop of pet-safe chamomile essential oil for a calming effect. Always check with your vet before adding new ingredients to your pet's diet.

Storage:

Store the dog treats in an airtight container in the refrigerator for up to 2 weeks. You can also freeze them for longer shelf life.

Oat and Pumpkin Pet Treats

Ingredients:

- 2 cups rolled oats
- 1/2 cup pure pumpkin puree (ensure it's not pumpkin pie filling)
- 1/4 cup water
- 1 tbsp dried parsley (optional for fresh breath)

Instructions:

1. Preheat your oven to 350°F (175°C).
2. Grind the rolled oats in a food processor until they reach a flour-like consistency.
3. In a large bowl, combine the oat flour with the pumpkin puree. Add water as needed to help the mixture come together.
4. Roll the dough into small, bite-sized balls or use a cookie cutter to create shapes.
5. Place the treats on a baking sheet lined with parchment paper.
6. Bake for 30 minutes or until the treats are dry and hard.
7. Let them cool completely before serving to your pet.

Oatmeal Treat for Cats

Ingredients:

- 1/2 cup rolled oats
- 1 cup water
- 1 tbsp finely chopped carrots
- 1 tbsp finely chopped spinach

Instructions:

1. In a saucepan, bring the water to a boil.
2. Add the rolled oats and simmer for about 10 minutes until the oats are soft.
3. Stir in the finely chopped carrots and spinach.
4. Allow the mixture to cool down.
5. Serve a small portion to your cat.

it's important to note that cats are obligate carnivores, which means their diet should primarily consist of meat. This recipe can be offered as an occasional treat, but should not replace a cat's regular diet.

Versatile Crop: Oats are not only used for human consumption but also for animal feed, particularly for horses. They are a valuable source of nutrition for livestock and are often fed to horses for their energy and digestive health benefits.

Birdie's Oat Buffet

Ingredients:

- 1 cup rolled oats
- 1/4 cup shelled sunflower seeds
- 1/4 cup millet
- 1/4 cup chopped almonds
- 1/4 cup dried cranberries

Instructions:

Mix all the ingredients in a bowl.

Serve in a clean bird feeder or sprinkle on a flat surface for ground-feeding birds.

Note: Always consult with a veterinarian before introducing new foods into your pet's diet to ensure they are safe and appropriate for your specific animal's health needs. Additionally, these recipes are intended as treats and should not replace a balanced diet tailored to your pet's species and individual requirements. Enjoy creating these wholesome treats for your furry and feathered friends!

Conclusion: The End of the Oat Rainbow: Final Thoughts

As we bring our oat exploration to a close, we celebrate the incredible journey we've embarked upon together. Through these pages, we've discovered the remarkable versatility of oats, transforming them from a simple grain into a myriad of delectable dishes. Your kitchen has become a canvas, and oats, the medium for your culinary artistry.

I am deeply grateful for your companionship on this voyage of oat discovery. Your passion for wholesome, oat-based cooking has been the inspiration behind each recipe crafted and every secret shared. It is my sincere hope that this cookbook has not only served as a guide but also as a spark for your own creative genius in the kitchen.

Now, I present to you the **DIY Oat Challenge**. Armed with the foundational recipes provided, I encourage you to unleash your imagination. Infuse these dishes with your personal flair—be it a sprinkle of your cherished herbs, a dash of exotic spices, or a lavish topping that speaks to your soul. Then, take to social media to share your oat-inspired creations. Tag this book, or leave a comment in the reviews with your innovative twists and turns. Go to my Facebook page and post pictures of your creations and recipes you have created. Let's create a community where our oat adventures can continue to grow and inspire.

Thank you for allowing oats to nourish your body, delight your palate, and inspire your heart. May your days be filled with the joy of discovery and the warmth of sharing your table with loved ones.

Here's to the endless possibilities that await in your kitchen and beyond. Keep the oat flame burning bright!

With heartfelt thanks and oats of love,

Beth Holm

beelovedholm@gmail.com

https://www.facebook.com/BethHolmAuthor

Sources: The Oat Library: A Kernel of Knowledge

1. Dr. Esselstyn's Prevent & Reverse Heart Disease Program | Make yourself heart attack proof. (n.d.). Retrieved June 11, 2024, from https://www.dresselstyn.com/site

2. Ornish Lifestyle Medicine. (n.d.). Ornish Lifestyle Medicine. https://www.ornish.com

3. Smart Nutrition, Superior Health. (2019). Drfuhrman.com. https://www.drfuhrman.com

4. Crawford, D. (2015). Center for Nutrition Studies. Center for Nutrition Studies. https://nutritionstudies.org

5. Greger, M. (2019). NutritionFacts.org. NutritionFacts.org. https://nutritionfacts.org

6. Dr. McDougall's Health & Medical Center. (2019). Drmcdougall.com. https://www.drmcdougall.comCollins, F. W. (2018). Avenanthramides in Oats: Antioxidant, Anti-inflammatory, and Other Benefits. *Journal of Cereal Science, 52*(2), 95-107.

7. U.S. Department of Agriculture. (n.d.). The Nutritional Value of Oats. USDA Nutritional Database. Retrieved from https://fdc.nal.usda.gov/fdc-app.html#/food-details/168435/nutrients

8. Whitehead, A., Beck, E. J., Tosh, S., & Wolever, T. M. (2014). Cholesterol-lowering effects of oat β-glucan: a meta-analysis of randomized controlled trials. *American Journal of Clinical Nutrition, 100*(6), 1413-1421.

9. Maki, K. C., Galant, R., Samuel, P., Tesser, J., Witchger, M. S., Ribaya-

10. Mercado, J. D., & Blumberg, J. B. (2007). Effects of consuming foods containing oat β-glucan on blood pressure: a randomized, controlled trial. *Journal of Nutrition, 137*(6), 1452-1455.

11. Slavin, J. L., & Green, H. (2007). Dietary fiber and satiety. *Nutrition Reviews, 65*(12), 285-291.

12. Reynertson, K. A., Garay, M., Nebus, J., & Rodriguez, D. (2015). Topical Oatmeal in Dermatology: A Review. *Journal of Drugs in Dermatology, 14*(6), 486-491.

13. Nwaru, B. I., Takkinen, H.-M., Niemelä, O., Kaila, M., Erkkola, M., Ahonen, S., & Kalliomäki, M. (2010). Timing of infant feeding in relation to childhood asthma and allergic diseases. *International Archives of Allergy and Immunology, 154*(3), 307-324.

Table of Contents

Books by Beth Holm

Wise and Thrifty Book Series

Budget Hacks: Practical Savings Strategies for Real People: Guide to Getting Ahead From a Frugal Mother of 8 That Did It on One Income

This comprehensive guide, born from the wisdom of a frugal mother of 8 who conquered financial challenges on a single income, unravels the secrets of achieving prosperity through the art of strategic living.

Beyond Oatmeal: Oats - The Impressive Superfood

Explore oats' incredible benefits, from sugar and oil-free treats to savory oat burgers. Packed with essential nutrients, oats support heart health, regulate blood sugar, and promote weight management. Beyond health benefits, discover economical meal ideas, gluten-free options, and heart-healthy choices.

Life's Tapestry Book Series

Reflections

A guided journal that encourages deep introspection and reflection on life, accomplishments, and personal growth. It aims to create a written legacy for future generations by providing thought-provoking questions and guidance on documenting reflections in an organized manner.

Made in the USA
Middletown, DE
29 July 2024

58123436R00099